D0287711

HD
9999
.U52
.R43
1993

WITHDRAWN

THE BEST AND THE REST
OF
REDDEN'S RULES OF THUMB

Almost 200 Money-Saving, Money-Making Tips
For the Cemetery/Mortuary Industry

J.C. Redden
President of Cemetery Mortuary Consultants, Inc.

The Lincoln-Bradley Publishing Group
New York
Memphis   Gatlinburg

Copyright © 1993 by J.C. Redden

Printed in the United States of America

All rights reserved. No part of this book may be reproduced or utilized in any form or by any means, electronic or mechanical, including photocopying, recording or by any information storage and retrieval system, without permission in writing from the Publisher, except by a reviewer who wishes to quote brief passages in connection with a review written for inclusion in a magazine, newspaper or broadcast. Inquires should be addressed to:

Permissions Department
The Lincoln-Bradley Publishing Group
P.O. Box 808
Gatlinburg, TN 37738

Publisher's Cataloging in Publication
(Quality Books, Inc.)

Redden, J.C.
   The best and the rest of Redden's rules of thumb:
almost 200 money-saving, money-making tips for the
cemetery/mortuary industry / J.C. Redden.
   p. cm.
   Includes bibliographical references and index.
   ISBN 1-879111-24-1

   1. Undertakers and undertaking—Vocational guidance.
2. Cemeteries—management. I. Title.

HD9999.U52R43 1993   363.75'068

                                             QBI93-934

Printed on approved acid-free paper
Book Design by Electronic Publishing Services, Inc.
1 2 3 4 5 6 7 8 9 10

Dedication

Almost all books are dedicated. Usually to the people that had to stand to the side while the writer wrote. The people we are closest to are also the ones who provided the encouragement needed.

The family consists of my wife Barbara, my son, John H. Redden and daughter, Judy Kenley. Also included are my sister, Eleanor Bathaltar and my niece Adrian Austen.

I have a great family. My work has always been dedicated to their welfare. This book is no place to change that.

My parents and sister, who have passed away, would have been proud.

The Best and the Rest of Redden's Rules of Thumb is available at special quantity discounts. For details regarding quantity purchases, write or telephone:

Special Markets
The Lincoln-Bradley Publishing Group
P.O. Box 808
Gatlinburg, TN 37738
(615) 436-4762

For additional inquiries, you may contact our above business office, or, according to your interests, you may contact us at:

Production Office
The Lincoln-Bradley Publishing Group
305 Madison Avenue – Suite 1166
New York, NY 10165
(212) 953-1125

Editorial Office
The Lincoln-Bradley Publishing Group
3780 S. Mendenhall Road – Suite 206
Memphis, Tennessee 38115
(901) 363-3518

TABLE OF CONTENTS

15   **Section II – Funeral**

Special Thanks

Steve Williford and his assistant, Louise Weigel, have performed well for me in putting this work together. Also, thank you to Publisher Carl Mays for his special attention and participation.

All of the staff at The Lincoln-Bradley Publishing Group really pitched in and led the way.

Also, special thanks to Dr. Billy Flatt, Dean of the Harding Graduate School of Religion, Memphis, Tennessee. He and I founded the Grief Recovery of Widowed Program at *Memorial Park*, Memphis, Tennessee, in 1976. That good work still goes on, with my son, John H. Redden, M.S., as the facilitator.

Foreword

I cannot say I have had an urge to put thoughts in book form.

I have written this book without that drive. The drive to write these thoughts came from a desire to leave something useful as I depart this life. There is no hurry for departure. I enjoy excellent health. At the age of 65 (though I know you don't think I look that old), the mind turns to eschatology, the last things.

Thoughts of the last things bring up thoughts of the years I have spent in the cemetery and funeral businesses. It began in 1952, at *Acacia Park* in Chicago. That was cemetery. The experiences in the funeral services started in 1970, and I was Executive Vice President of *Memorial Park* in Memphis; the funeral home was built on that cemetery in 1977.

Life continues to be productive, rewarding and, yes, enjoyable. In 1982, we at *Memorial Park* formed a consulting company. In 1988, I mysteriously acquired all the stock of the consulting company and embarked on my dream to be the best there is in that field. I have found I am good at what I do, but I do not charge enough money. My clients are too satisfied.

The material that follows is far from deep, but a lot of it has a spin on it that reflects the capsule of my thinking.

This book is designed to be used. The new person in either the cemetery or funeral service will find aid and direction. The operator in the funeral service will find the information regarding the cemetery work to be useful. The same is said for the cemeterian looking at the funeral business.

The Table of Contents is a Topic Index and the index in the back of the book is a Word Index.

All the work herein is from my experiences and, therefore, from the people I have had the pleasure of working with through the years. I listed some of them at the back of the book in the "Peopleography." Those not mentioned, and there will be many, I have stated to have been subtle in their teachings. More accurately, I *strove* to list all, realizing some would go unlisted.

'Tis noble to forgive, so be noble.

Section I

CEMETERY

Q   Should I purchase a cemetery or should I start one from scratch?

A   The least expensive move is usually to start a cemetery from scratch. However, if the short term or moderately short term plan includes a funeral home, the most efficient method would be to acquire a cemetery. This is true, since the lot owners would be available as leads for the pre-need funeral sale. Also, the same heritage is useful for contact for sales completing the lot owner's needs with such items as pre-need memorials, vaults and opening and closing charges. Current lot owners are the best source for referrals, names of other family and close friends that may not have selected cemetery property. Short term, the likelihood of a funeral home being constructed on a cemetery is not high. Yet, in an area where the pre-need law is friendly, or where we have "full" cemeteries for competition, it is a possibility. A friendly pre-need law is one where the solicitation of pre-need funerals is not prohibited, and even friendlier is the law that permits the provider enough net revenue to fund the sales activity desired.

There *are* occasions where existing properties can be purchased for even less money down than it would take to buy the raw land. In that event, the zoning problem would have been handled ahead of time and likely a minimal investigation would determine that the land is useable for cemetery property. When purchasing an existing cemetery that is quite well developed and sold, obviously the questions of adjacent land options and land availability become an issue.

Q   What is the maximum I can spend for land and still be able to be profitable?

A   If my goal is to strive for 30% profit before taxes in the cemetery operation, and my expenses run 35% and my costs run 35%, the land cost should be no more than 10% of the 35% cost figure.

Figure it out. We assume 1000 spaces per acre, net after roads and other improvements and features, using a 3.5' x 9' space. A $1000.00 space will require a profit of $300.00. Costs at 35% are needed to buy the wholesale memorial and/or the vault.

The land maximum should be $35.00, preferably $30.00 ($30,000.00 per acre for the land provides a space at $30.00). The costs (35%) total $350.00. In order to get the land cost inside the $35.00 cost budget figure, the purchase of merchandise (memorials, vaults, for example) will need tight control. On the financials, of course, the issues are separated as the costs will show up as short term liabilities and the land as inventory in the form of an asset. Here we have presented some more stuff that is up for argument. There is not a whole lot of argument if you are setting up your sales for the full package of the lot, memorial, opening and closing and the vault. When you see the author in the hall and you want to disagree with him on this one, remember all the things your mother taught you (courtesy, etc.).

Q What is the annual cost to cut and trim an acre of the typical cemetery?

A The cost will be 1/10th of grounds operations. If grounds operations were $500,000.00 on 100 acres, the cost per year is $5000.00 per acre per year. Using a $6.00 per hour labor (who is that fortunate?), the cost of cutting and trimming is $422.40. The 100 acre figure is $42,240.00. Rounding off like that is how we get a rule of thumb.

Q How many men should be on the grounds crew? What is the rule of thumb?

A One person full time for each 50 interments per year. Therefore, 500 interments = 10 people. Want to argue about that one? Do your own research, using the criteria that *excellence* is the standard. Variables abound. The point is, too many of my colleagues do not have a handle on grounds costs. They do not take the time to establish ratios and rules of thumb from which to work.

Q How many spaces in an acre?

A Twenty percent of an undeveloped acre will be dedicated to roads and landscaping. On monument lots, three and a half by ten feet (3½' x 10') spaces; on non-monument lots, three and a half by nine feet (3½' x 9'); and on lawns crypt sections three feet by eight feet (3' x 8'). Effective ways to waste money are to have too many roads, thus using more of the land than you have to and having too large a space. One more way is to have paths.

Q How can I expand the limited land for a cemetery?

A Through the use of garden crypts, mausoleum crypts and multiple depth interments. Ordinarily, land is available on the perimeter of a cemetery. Therefore, "perimeter crypts" would go a long way toward expanding the use of land. Traditional single burial use of land is one to one. Typically, a four to one ratio is developed where the mausoleum crypt runs up to eight crypts high. Coming onto the scene is the "chamber crypt" wherein the units are 10' high and all under the surface. Corridors are there for the placement of the casket, but the areas are non-visitation, with the memorialization arranged for above the surface.

Want more? How about renting space, and in 30 years cremating the remains and placing them in a wall niche? All of this you had arranged at the time of the first sale. Enough of that dreaming. On the other hand, the lawn crypt had a beginning. So did the community mausoleum crypt. The issue is, who will figure out how to market new ideas? More. The author built a unit of reduced size crypts 40% smaller than the usual crypt. Therefore, a casket is not used. A fiber glass tube is. Let's not even try to touch the land use of the inurnment (an urn garden) and interment of cremated remains. The best use of land, bar none.

Q Why or why not have monuments?

A If the marketplace in past history has required monuments, you should have monuments as a choice. As memorial parks mature, they tend to add monument sections. In the beginning, memorial parks sold a new idea, bronze lawn level markers, where the traditional cemetery sold monuments. Now, we want to broaden our lines. We provide granite and let the resulting open competition have its effect. It would be good business to consider a joint venture with the local monument dealer. Better yet, he may well be for sale. If your area does not use monuments, there is little reason to introduce them, outside of the very important cost issue. As the copper and bronze costs escalate and sur charges (temporary) are added, the granite becomes more attractive.

Q   What is the approximate cost per acre to develop a cemetery?

A   Assuming it's a new cemetery, today's cost will dictate a minimum of $20,000.00 per acre to develop a cemetery. Only a fool would put that number on paper. Yet, given we do not select a rock quarry or a marsh for a cemetery site, you can predict a rough idea of the cost. Developing a new section in a location with the roads already in place will not require near as large a per acre development cost. Individual sections, on the other hand, may require substantial earth moving and/or dirt removal or addition.

Now for the rest of the story. Section widths, road design, features, soft beds, amount developed at the outset, degree of elegance and the cost of the theme of the cemetery. The what? The theme. Never start a cemetery without the establishment of an excuse for its existence for reasons other than that of a burial site. A grotto, a waterfall, a museum, the section depicting the life of the Christ, etc.

Oh yes, I almost forgot the curbs. Likely, we will have some. I have seen properties that have all the sections curbed. Then, what style curb? Except at the front of the property, no curbs are needed. Style? Well, don't use bricks on end for curbs. Ever see one of those? I have, and the lot owner seems to be unable to avoid them. Cut tires. A good idea is the swail or gutter curb. Keeps the car off the grass and aids in the flow of water.

Q   Should cemetery roads be concave or convex?

A   The road should be concave, thus moving the storm water down the center of the road and into the sewers at the intersections. Crowned roads waste land at the roadside and/or force installation of drain tiles. Recently, I established a five acre section. Good design and minimal road construction costs. Too few design people have the costs of operations in their hearts as they spend your dollars. Concave roads save dollars and move water.

Q   What factors control the location of the land I select for a cemetery?

A   Other than zoning, marketing factors and basic land costs, soil conditions are critical issues. Boring should be done on 400' centers to depths of 8'. These borings will reveal soil make-up and show where rock or high water tables will prohibit interments. There is no zoning for a cemetery. This means a variation in the existing zoning is needed. It is usually wise when seeking a site for the establishment of a cemetery to look for land adjacent to a long established church yard cemetery or some other rural cemetery. Here, the zoning issue is settled. I think it was three years ago the American Cemetery Association issued a book regarding the planning of a cemetery. A very good piece of work headed by Dave Hunt.

Q   In zoning a cemetery, what reactions are to be expected?

A   Resistance from all levels. Since resistance is expected, it should not prevent the project. Where cemeteries are located outside the populous area, there are multitudes of examples that show that developments will build around the cemetery. The cemetery then becomes a "Green Belt," letting the new neighbors know nothing else will be built there. That information helps sway boards and zoning commissions to permit the zoning variance.

Q   How do I determine the selling cost of a cemetery lot?

A   The price should be competitive on the high side to begin with as you start your "Founders Group." A "Founders Group" is a promotion where you provide the best of everything, selection and price, to the original purchasers. The promotion is attractive enough to create a desire in the prospective purchasers mind to get in the new program before it is shut off and the purchase becomes less beneficial. If my average competition had a cemetery lot for sale at $600, I might well price mine at $800 and offer a "Founders Group discount" of $100, giving a net sale of $700. As the section matures and we go to another section, discounts are minimized.

To have a "Beautification Division" in the grounds operations is to provide a formal garden, for example, or to plant, in season, annuals and perennials. This makes my cemetery a true show place. I will have to charge more than is typical in the marketplace. I would in that case have to charge what is necessary to be decently profitable plus the costs of this special division. In any marketing scheme, the choice to go low or high in the price at the outset is ours. The nature of man is such that we can well charge more, offer benefits for the pre-need sale and still end up netting more than the competition. People will always buy the best. Since our product is sold, not bought, the pre-need sale and its features are the things that will carry the day. We need to be on the high side, not go in low.

Q   How do I determine the retail price of cemetery products and services?

A   Price formulas on mausoleum crypts usually vary according to location of the crypt, the tiers constructed and the type of crypt unit. Garden and mausoleum crypts need to be coordinated with the price of the full land package. Half of the crypt inventory must overlap the total price of the land package of lot, memorial, vault and opening and closing. Of course, the elegance of the design and use of materials will affect the price.

On average, a price on a crypt should be three and a half times the construction costs, including landscaping. The top two tiers should be a full percentage less. On average, the pricing for a monument or a memorial, taking into consideration all issues, should permit us to have a three time mark-up on that product. Interment service retail charges should be four to six times the true full costs. After the ground sale, the best profit is derived from the lawn crypt and the garden crypt products. The garden unit has the advantage of providing more dollars. Again, this ignores the niche sales. This should always be the best profit item. The obvious problem is the market's acceptance of cremation and the presence of direct disposal firms.

Q   What is the rule of thumb for section widths?

A   Traditionally, a section would be no more than 400' wide, thus permitting ease of casket carrying for the pallbearers. As costs move up, this is no longer true. Narrow sections require too many roads. The rule now could easily provide for a 500' wide section as opposed to 400'.

Q   How do I find a sales manager?

A First, avoid the time honored theft of your competition's sales manager. Then, toss the dice and contact the state and local associations. They provide a better and more honorable way. Some employ sales contractors. These firms should be operations that contract in our businesses only. Care needs to be taken as you deal with a contractor for your pre-need efforts to clearly understand your costs and the flow of cash on the sale. Find people who are skilled professionals in sales management and train them in our products and services. While this is not done much in the cemetery business, it is a viable solution. This project should be done also by a consultant. The exception is obviously in the employment of a sales contractor. Contractors must know our work (*See Appendix B*).

Q How do I figure out a price for my cemetery?

A Fair market value is defined as a situation where a knowledgeable buyer and a knowledgeable seller, both motivated, are interested in the transaction. That is a paraphrase of the accepted standard. God forbid I should provide you with the exact language. Go to an expert. The typical cemeterian cannot objectively put a price on his own operations. He has too much of himself in the property and may well price the property too high. Again, a knowledgeable consultant will be able to help with this situation.

A simple approach of having an appraisal cannot get the job done, since there are very few neighborhood transactions that set the pace for the price of a cemetery. Generally, they are too complex to be priced with a simple formula. Of course, it is true, small corporations usually are bought and sold for a price acceptable to each party regardless of the ability to justify the price. The expert will serve another purpose. Perhaps you don't sell and the property goes into your estate. At what value? The independent valuation will satisfy this situation. *Your* price or your CPA's is not acceptable to the IRS.

Q If we put an interment in the wrong site, what rights do we have to correct the error?

A Your rules and regulations must enable the directors of a corporation to permit management to correct errors. An error once made in a cemetery frequently cannot be changed through erasure, but must be changed by some very dramatic work.

Correct the error and then notify the property owners of the error and its correction. That is a controversial statement. So, I hasten to urge you to contact your attorney. If he does not agree with what I have said here, be certain he understands that the error may well have taken place on two sites owned by families. To notify first is to face an impasse and the high possibility of an impasse and litigation.

Q   Is tight control over lead flow a good strategy?

A   Tight control over high producers usually backfires. Tight control over the average and lower producers costs money and may well not be worth the dollars and energy. Maybe we should confine tight control to a certain brand of leads such as those generated by the company. Otherwise the rule, "He who writes gets," is wise. That means if a person writes an agreement, that person receives the commission. No jury trials. Some of the age lines I show in my photos are from trying to settle commission disputes in my early career. You never please both. So, in those cases, I have learned the following process:

1. He who writes gets.

2. If that doesn't do it, the parties to the dispute have to settle the matter between themselves by payroll cut-off, or

3. He who writes gets.

Q   What are some reliable numbers in the sales end of our business pre-need?

A   Try the formula: 35-10-6-2. That would translate into 35 contacts a day (which will probably require 70 attempts). This will on a weekly basis produce 10 appointments, six presentations and two sales. Here are some more numbers. One hundred leads are needed to maintain a decent inventory. Also, in every 15 qualified leads there is one immediate sale.

In recruiting, 15 responses to an ad (15 is a normal first day response), equals 10 appointment interviews. This will result in six kept appointments for the interview, which will result in four hires. Ninety days later, one of the four will still be on your staff. The key here is to carefully screen the people, using psychological tests and credit checks, plus asking the question of the former employer, "Would you rehire this person?" The problem with numbers is that they work when the people having access to them work. Very few counselors will put in a 40 hour week.

If I had six presentations and each presentation took two hours (including travel), I would have used up 12 hours in that week. Generally, it will require three hours of prospecting to talk to 35 people. That comes to fifteen hours a week using a five day week. So, 27 hours dedicated to prospecting and presentations. Planning and paperwork will add another five hours a week. This leaves eight hours of a 40 hour week for more presentations and prospecting. Really strong sales producers put in far more than a 40 hour week. People who are pure "closers" put in less and people weak to average also put in too little time. I would suggest the above numbers should be used as standard or a plan, and then set out to prove or disprove those numbers and in the process establish your own numbers.

Q   Should salespeople be employees or independent contractors?

A   Keep in mind that if you choose the independent contractor route and can't adhere to the guidelines as laid out by IRS, you are subject to going back in time to the beginning of your decision to payment of Social Security. While cost of operations may well be increased by providing full benefits, in the long run, you will keep your salespeople longer if they are employees versus independent contractors.

Q   What benefits can I afford to pay cemetery sales counselors?

A   'Tis truly a shame that this question makes sense. Owners resist the payment of benefits to salespeople. Less so when they are productive. Paying sales counselors the same benefits paid to other employees is the right thing to do. Actually, you can better afford to pay the counselors those benefits if they are producers. It is possible to withhold, provided that certain levels of performance are achieved by counselors. It is also possible once they have achieved those levels, to pay partial or full benefits depending on monthly volume. Another controversial topic. My feeling is the turnover is lessened as the people are part of the firm, employees. The interviewing, testing and training has to be on a higher level than in the case of hiring an independent contractor.

Q   What are the major pitfalls of the family service approach?

A   Family service people deal with families having interment arrangements to make. They help them with details prior to the service and schedule post-funeral visits. They also encourage future pre-need sales to avoid future anxiety and trauma.

In the first place, the pre-need division resents the family service approach. That having been said, another pitfall is family service people tend to become social workers. Their service motive and case load frequently prevent much in the way of pre-need sales volume. Even those people who start out fast to produce revenue in pre-need sales through family service tend to tail off as their case loads increase. Social workers do not write contracts. Family service people lose sight of the fact that the greatest aid they can render a family is to sell them.

Better, advise them and "insist" on their carrying out the obligation they have to protect the survivors. The rule of thumb is seven families a month, which includes all of the pre and post interment needs. Competition for the duty is a key to waking up pre-need production. Those that do not qualify in a given month fall back on their other lead sources in order to gain duty again (*See Appendix A*).

Q   Should a counselor be permitted to sell everything or should I have separate groups for the different products?

A   The training for a counselor should be on simple levels and grow as he/she produces on the simple levels. The ultimate is that your counselor can handle any product or service available on a pre-need basis. It is more efficient to have separate divisions, but it is not wise for the customer to be passed from one counselor to another. Taking the best possible care of the customer is, after all, the right thing to do. Sometimes the state law takes care of this for you. Perhaps you cannot sell a funeral pre-need without a license.

Q   Should I hire part time salespeople?

A   While I would discourage it, I would never say never. Every effort should be made to not hire part time people. It is possible to hire part time people with one task only at the outset: that they are prospectors and their job is to turn leads until they can make a decision as to whether or not to go full time.

Q Which are more effective in the pre-need sale, men or women?

A Women whose children are raised and gone are every bit as effective and, in many cases, more effective than men in the pre-need sale. My experience: Women who have small children at home generally, even though they accept the job, run into difficulties with guilt and husbands. The safe approach might be to hire those whose children are at least high school age. Which are more effective has a lot to do with the records you have experienced. There is no research that settles the issue.

Q How deep is a grave?

A While much might depend on whether or not the backhoe operator had an argument with his wife that morning, a grave for an interment will leave 18" to 24" of earth compacted above the burial receptacle. Therefore, the height of the container dictates the depth of the grave. Less earth on top of the receptacle will impede the growth of the sod.

Q How wide should a grave be and why is that true?

A It should be wider than the outside dimension of a receptacle. The obvious exception would be where pre-poured lawn crypts are installed in volume. A safe width is 3½' with a 3' opening in a traditional section. The fact that the width of a back hoe bucket can be 36" brings up the question of the chicken or the egg.

Q What is the proper grave length?

A Monument lots should have a 10' grave. Non-monument property can use more comfortably a nine foot grave. Eight foot grave lengths are frequently the case where lawn crypts are pre-poured. Where markers are pre-installed or, of course, installed on a first interment in a lawn crypt double depth area, an eight foot grave requires that the marker is removed. A section 500' wide using a 10' grave in non-monument sites wastes land, loses money and lessens the deposits to the endowments care trust. Would you believe a loss of 3.5' for each of the 50 spaces across the section? Now, the length of the section is factored in as is the price in that section.

Q How high can you build garden crypts and still have a saleable product?

A You need to be able to see the lettering. I have not seen any higher than 10 tiers. Of course, there are developments where crypts are six or seven high and then set back into a slope and a staircase built up with a walkway in front of the crypts on the second tier. In a case like that, it could well be that you would have 20 crypts high.

Q Should I sell the opening and closing pre-need?

A Yes. The money should all go into investments. Some state laws require percentages of pre-need sales of any product or service to be deposited under a "merchandise law" in the state cemetery code. In any event, as time goes on and we are challenged in the sale of the opening and closing, it is much better to have locked it in through the pre-need sale. Further, it is true that the money will earn money on a compounded basis faster than it will be subject to inflation delivery.

Wanting to save the opening and closing for the income needed at the time of the interment is a great reason for pre-selling it. The question then is simply, in whose bank shall it be saved, the lot owners or the company? If you have it, it is off the mind of the customer and is out of his assets. You should get a copy of the Wyatt Report. Published in 1991, this report, commissioned by the Pre-Arrangement Association, shows the relationship of investments to inflation and cemetery and funeral home costs over a 20 year period, 1970-1990.

Q What should not be sold pre-need?

A Any product or service supplied to the lot owner eventually should be sold pre-need. Exception. This may not happen at the same time. During times of construction of garden units, for example, the Opening/Closing may be withheld on the landsale to help promote crypt sales.

Q What is the actual cost of a cremation?

A Usually a lot of revenue. A study in any given operation of the labor, fuel and deprecation will finally determine the actual cost of a cremation. Obviously, when cremating in a non-combustible container, there is a different cost factor because of time necessary to cremate and handle the remains.

Q At what point should I have a crematory?

A When you can afford it. The truth is, very few crematories start up in a profitable mode and very few become profitable. In a market where cremation is 30% of deaths, much cremation work is already done in the area and your adding a crematory might not have any beneficial impact to the corporation except to have a full service organization.

Q How wide is a cemetery road?

A In the entrance area, a boulevard is a suggested approach and each side of the boulevard should be 22' wide. Into the cemetery the primary roads should be 18' wide, and tertiary roads can be 16' wide. Think cul-de-sacs. This is a good way to save road costs. But, they still will not be wide enough to keep all the people off. Once, I had just paved a road in Forest Hill in Memphis. As we placed the final barrier in front of the fresh blacktop a "person" swung around it and drove right up on the new stuff. While that has nothing to do with width, it is a good true story and makes a point. Despair not. You will bury that type person some day.

Q How steep a slope can be tolerated in maintenance of a cemetery with power equipment?

A A 20 degree slope is the maximum that can be tolerated and maintain safe operations. Obviously, since that's the maximum, it should be avoided and substituted by the lower maximum of a 15 degree slope for purposes of safety. This is a question of the planning phase that needs attention. One could test this premise by falling off equipment and then determining the slope degree at which the fall took place. Perhaps your son-in-law could help here.

Q What degree slope must I maintain as the section and the road meet in the cemetery?

A A one and one half degree slope is a minimum. Clearly, the water must move off the section onto the road without standing. What must be avoided at all costs is that the section, as it approaches the road, is flat or lower than the road. When that is allowed to happen, water undermines edges of the road. In a cold climate the problem is compounded by a freeze.

Q How do I best control commission costs?

A By insisting upon production in order to gain maximum commissions. Commissions should not be the same for every sale at any time of the month. They should be lower on early volume and higher on later volume, with the proper goals achieved bringing up the commission on the lower volume sales. This avoids the obvious problem of a low producer making high percentage commissions on low production. That is very costly to the operation. If your son-in-law is making his wife work as he sells for you, he needs less money to survive and thus gets by on a deal where you pay high commission for each sale. For example, pay the man 10% on the first $10,000.00 production in the month. Then, pay him 1% for each additional $1000.00 he produces in that month. There is a need for a LID. Place the highest LID on the product you are most interested in selling.

Q Is it legal to scatter cremated remains?

A Generally, yes; and always it's true if the scattering is done inside a cemetery under auspices of the cemetery management. The number of states that permit cremated remains to be scattered by stating such in the law remains at zero, as far as I know. Some states specifically prohibit the scattering of cremated remains. A study of your state law will let you know the current situation.

Section II

Funeral

Q What percent costs of the funeral income dollar should personnel be?

A At maximum, 25%. Well now, here we go again with the in-laws and the self. Those are likely officer's compensation and are a separate issue. The operating personnel, otherwise, should not exceed the 25% figure. Maybe your father-in-law can be "gotten" for less, especially if he gets a title.

Q What percent costs of the funeral income dollar should the merchandise be; for example, the casket?

A Fifteen percent maximum. Mark-up on a vault may not be as great as on the casket. Other merchandise items are not critical issues. That will change in areas where the casket store competes. The services will be the greater of those charges.

Q How do I determine the number of square feet to build in the funeral home to start?

A Depending upon local custom, the visitation room may be the "social gathering place." Rule of thumb is one visitation room for each 150 funerals per year. The typical funeral chapel will seat 250 people. Public corridors in the funeral home should be 10 or 12 feet wide. Service corridors behind the staterooms need not be more than six to eight feet wide.

Do a pro forma that tells you how many interments will be converted to funerals in the first year, the second year, the third year, etc. That will let you know how many staterooms to build, on a "modular" basis (see your consultant). In some cases, the visitation rooms (slumber rooms) double as the chapel. I would not advise trying to gain that construction cost advantage if this double use of the facility is not the custom in your area. Research it first (consultant again). (*See Appendix D*).

Q What is an expectable profit-before-tax margin in a "typical" funeral home?

A Strive for 40%. This is outside the net proceeds of the pre-arrangement sale. If you do not achieve this 40%, you are likely afraid of the competition (paranoia). The solution is in the casket price. As the "casket store" becomes more of an issue, the traditional funeral director will have to consider switching the major profit from the casket to the services. What the casket store does, does **not** change your obligation to be profitable. So far, the casket store people are apt to be former high casket sale producers with traditional funeral homes. (*Irony. This book is the sole source of this figure. No one wants to declare, in print, that 40% is achievable. Maybe I don't want to either.*)

Q What is an expectable profit before taxes in a "typical" cemetery operation?

A Since a funeral home is a cash operation and a cemetery is full of contingent liabilities, the "typical" profit before taxes of a cemetery will be less than the funeral home's, but should not be tolerated under 30%. Cemeterians know how to sell the products pre-need and at-need. Too often they operate off the check book balance and have only a vague idea of what their profit performance is. Elaborate audits are filed and not read. This is true where audits are done. The fellow who does not do an audit may not be worse off, but he also has a reason for not doing a thorough job on cost control and profit. He simply has no way of knowing.

Q How do I figure out the price for my funeral home?

A Rules of thumb are talked about, such as four or five times earnings over the past five years. As is the case with rules of thumb, this establishes little more than a starting place or a number to bounce off of. People in the business of acquisitions can look at the financials of a funeral home and in little or no time, come up with a figure. Generally, the process is pretty much the same as the answer for pricing any retail business. Differences lie in the need for a special license and the training that goes with the license. Otherwise, most retail businesses have trained personnel and merchandise to buy and sell. The name of the firm may well be thought to be more important in the funeral business than in other retail businesses. This may or may not be true. The real estate and its location is an issue factored into the price. Formal valuations are possible. The consultant can handle this.

Q How many licensed personnel should I count on having to hire to properly handle the case load?

A Rule of thumb, one licensed person can handle 100 funerals. That full time person would then be backed up on 100 cases by two part time people working an average one-half work week each. In-laws can well change this in either direction. As can the favorite non-relative employee.

Q Do funeral directors have an effective following in the community?

A As time goes on and as cemeterians become more involved in funeral services, they need to take a lesson from the funeral director in establishing more close and consistent contacts with the community. Frequently, other than going to church and perhaps Rotary, cemeterians do not involve themselves nearly enough in the community. As cemeteries mature, this issue becomes more important. As more of the sales volume comes from the family service approach to the sales, the need to be involved in the community is of greater importance.

Few state legislatures have cemeterians as members. Frequently, legislatures have funeral directors in both houses at any given time. Our future is in the hands (partially) of the state legislatures. Community involvement is the way into service as a legislator. And that is a great and beneficial service.

Q Is a "combination" funeral home a depleting asset, as is a cemetery?

A Think with me on this one. If it is the case that 95% of the funerals serviced by a combination will be buried in that cemetery, then it has to be a depleting asset. The timing is not the same; an average of 30 years will go by before that property sale turns into a funeral. As your pre-need site sales exceed the rate of interment, the funeral is a growing asset. But, at some future point, the funeral home on the cemetery has to produce a declining caseload. So, if you think the funeral home on the cemetery is an insurance policy on the life of the cemetery, you are, short term, right. Long term, the only way that can happen is where the public uses your combination funeral home and buries in a different cemetery. That is a good one for cemetery trivia, since that "fact" takes too long to prove and this is now.

Q   How many dollars should go to advertising the combination cemetery/funeral home?

A   Another rule of thumb. Over the first 12 months, 10% of the cost of the structure. Example: $1,000,000.00 to build the building equal $100,000.00 in advertising. After that, a normal percent of revenues, say 2.5%. The entire community needs to know that if they had lots at your place, there is a funeral home there. So, buy lots with us. Since the premise is, again, you will bury in your cemetery 95% of the funerals you handle, your target is the lot owner. Your efforts shall be in the form of zeroing in on the needs, wishes and education of the lot owner.

Grief

Author's note: I have been interested in grief recovery for many years. As a licensed and degreed counselor, and having performed hundreds of grief recovery sessions for our industry, I share the following questions and answers. I hope they prove practical and useful.

Q   Does grief ever go away?

A. Grief is love. Neither love nor grief can go away as long as there is a memory of the loved one. In time and through the healing processes built into the human, we function better. But, ten years later, out of nowhere, the pain and tears can rush back, then leave, only to return.

Q   How long does intense grief last?

A   Birthdays of all concerned, holidays, anniversaries, church, all those things the loved ones experienced together have to be experienced alone for the first time. So, the pain usually is intense for at least a year. There are exceptions. The next six months continue to offer very little change. Somewhere in there, however, the griever starts to reach out, move better, cry less, smile more. The answer is, the process is likely to last 18 months, plus or minus. Since good and bad days come and go without warning, you will hear a griever claim to be going crazy. Well, crazy is normal (in this sense) for a griever.

Q   What is a griever expecting to receive from the funeral director?

A   Empathetic efficiency. No tears, no gushiness. You are not in their ball park. To empathize is to show a concern for their situation. You never, *never* tell them you understand, even if you have experienced the death of loved ones very close to you. Their case is special and they resent you saying you understand when the widow knows you cannot understand her special case.

Q   Is the funeral therapeutic?

A   Yes. World wide, the process of gathering together, hugging and crying, points up the value of celebrating the life in the short span of the funeral ritual. However, we in this work err if we think there is long term therapeutic value in the funeral. Soon, it is a point in time, almost unidentified in conversations, unless something went wrong at the time of the funeral. In a case like that, the funeral is remembered as just one more thing. about the situation that hurts. But that is not therapy.

Q   Is the funeral director a therapist?

A   No. Nor do I think they think they should be. I have heard some of the "famous" on the grief speaking circuit almost come out and say the funeral director is a therapist. Their logic is that if by definition the funeral is therapeutic, then he who directs it is a therapist.

Q   What can we do to benefit the griever?

A   Put the person with someone who has been there. In this post death time, we are able to help by doing the obvious. Provide groups, lists of community resources designed to aid the griever. Visit them soon after the service and then stay in touch. Your family service people should be good card writers. Have your staff trained in the post death grief process. I provide such training and am available for on-site seminars.

Q   How do the grounds people need to face the grief issue?

A   How often does the thought cross your mind that the most consistent contact with the griever is the ground personnel? Scare you? They should be trained in the amount of knowledge needed to understand what this crabby lot owner is all about. They will then do an even better job of fixing complaints. Be sure your grounds people are dressed in uniform. Neat as possible given the circumstances. This is a good place to mention the need to keep the grounds and the equipment up to a high standard. If you contemplate a funeral home on the cemetery, or if you already have one, you find that how you handle complaints and the appearance of equipment and grounds to be directly connected to being favored with subsequent funeral services from your customer base.

Q   What is the family service person's responsibility?

A   In style or manner, not unlike the funeral director's. The work itself is confined to the cemetery arrangements in the usual situation. Empathy. Efficient and fast dispatch of the paper work involved and a careful review of the lot location, the specific space and section. Note the relationship of the interment to those interred on the lot.

Previously I've addressed other responsibilities. Some family service personnel appear at the funeral home visitation, the gravesite, and even lead in the funeral. The post funeral contact is arranged for and the family service person makes that call some three days after the interment. Being aware of the need for memorials and more spaces is not only important for the sake of the family, but also critical to the family service person, since that individual's compensation usually is tied to sales volume. The tendency of that family service person to dislike the sale hurts the program. The best way to help the family is to advise them to take care of the balance of their needs, now. Also, there is a need to get the rest of the family into the pre-arrangements for themselves. Again, family service people sometimes shy away from this responsibility. That cannot be tolerated in an organization where the goal is to be of maximum aid to the survivors.

Q   Does the sale affect the grief?

A   Put it this way. Never will you find a widow who thought the fact that she had pre-arrangements was a bad or foolish thing. On the other side, many many widowed persons who had not pre-arranged, state openly that they wish they had done so. To that extent, there is an impact on the grief. This beneficial impact does not greatly affect the grief experience. There is a help here, but it is not possible to measure since the person involved did not do one of each. She did or did not pre - arrange. The agony of the death-shopping trip would have been eliminated. Yet, exactly how much grief that would have eliminated is not known.

Section III

COMBINATION

Q   What is the best way to track production?

A   Poorly worded question. I mean, what time segments produce the best results. Count volume by the week. Then, be sure you pay by the week. Develop the additional practice of dividing personal earnings needs or goals into weekly segments. The fact that your salesperson sold $10,000.00 in one week does not do as much for him as the fact that he earned "x" dollars. This is, of course, in private. It should be done, since low turnover and high incomes go hand in hand.

Q   What is the best way to track counselor performance?

A   First, hire only people that report the truth on the report forms. Since one cannot be sure they have done that, read the rest of the comment. Daily reports on contacts, appointments, presentations and sales. The manager then converts these to a weekly summary report. These reports need review with the counselor by the sales coach.

Accountability. Do you remember the concentration you experienced as you were about to account for your behavior with any superior and some peers? Counselors do more, as they know they will have to back up the numbers. If you as the manager are not willing to go over the reports personally, on a weekly basis with each counselor, then do not have a written report system. Wing it.

Q   Who do I know that makes money on a greenhouse operation in a cemetery?

A   Directly, no one. Yet, that may be in part due to the fact that few ran close figures on the greenhouse. The greenhouse performed the function of special attention to the soft beds in the cemetery. Ultimately, you will get out of the cemetery greenhouse operation and buy wholesale or contract for the growing and placement.

Q   What is the biggest employee complaint of most corporations?

A   The problem is, "I don't know what's going on, and/or I don't have any input into what's going on." It's almost never money or working conditions.

Q   Is it solvable?

A   Not really. Concerted attempts to set up communication systems in a corporation that allow access to decision making and provides information to the employee about what's going on are absorbed and the complaint remains. They become accustomed to having input and accustomed to knowing what's going on and still feel that they don't know what's going on and don't have input. The amount of input and information provided is, therefore, absorbable by the employee. He gets accustomed to it and wants more.

Q   How do I protect myself against "Disgruntled Employee" problems?

A   When a person is hired, there should be a screening process by at least a second interview. People should then be tested if they are semi-skilled or skilled employees. The preparation for protection is in the hiring. The documentation issued at the time of employment should state basic corporate policies. The evidence of the understanding of the policy is demonstrated through the signature by the employee on a form containing the policies. Periodic evaluation done with the employee is another guard against disgruntled people. Evaluate and have the employee sign the evaluation form. File the evidence that the evaluation was performed and understood.

Q   In a joint operation, should the overall manager be a funeral director or cemeterian?

A   A cemeterian. Until another generation of funeral directors is developed wherein his training includes the value, the techniques and the benefits of the pre-need sale, the funeral director's thinking will not be aggressive enough to support pre-need operations. There are rare exceptions to this.

Q   Where should I locate a funeral home in a cemetery?

A   When possible, in an area that would gain the greatest exposure from the road. Over any period of time the public driving in front of a cemetery will notice a mortuary is located in that cemetery. That would at least account for some segment of the population knowing the funeral home is there. Do not expect the location to have a big impact on the case load. The public will believe the funeral home on the cemetery is for the lot owners. So, while I would put the building at the street, it would not be extremely detrimental if I could not do that. There are circumstances when one may well have a chance at "street" business for the funeral home at the cemetery location. For example, if my interment count were low I would consider street business as something to strive for when I had a statute that permitted net revenue at the point of a pre-need sale. I may well go ahead with the funeral home and put it either across the street or on an adjacent piece of land. In these cases, I would likely not use the cemetery name in the name of the funeral home.

Q   Do my people sell funerals, trusts, or insurance?

A   First, become aware of IRS's position on funeral trusts. You would sell funeral trusts in a state where the trust requirements are from 50 to 80%. In other cases, an insurance product should be used to fund the funeral sale. Obviously, ages or health conditions can affect the insurance sale and require, instead, annuities or trusts. One must be careful of the state law in this regard.

Q   How many interments should I have before starting a funeral home on the cemetery?

A   It is said the average case load for a funeral home in the USA is at the 100 level. For our purposes, we will call them all profitable ventures. I will, based on the following observations, need at least 200 interments. The probable maximum funerals achievable for a combination funeral home/cemetery, on site, is 75% of the interment count. This will take ten to fifteen years to achieve. This is 75% of the "useable" count of interments. If 50% of the interments are of a different race, whether or not those people will use your funeral home as easily as they use your cemetery has to be studied.

For the purpose of this question, let us assume the interment count is all useable. The first year the funeral home is in operation, we may look to fifteen percent of the interments using your combination funeral home in year one. Then, add five percent the second year. Let's assume further that we add five percent for each subsequent year. We will have 60% of the interment count at the end of ten years and the target 75% at the end of thirteen years. All this is done without counting on "street" business or pre-need revenues. At this point, we suggest a fudge factor and come up with the "Rule of Thumb."

A friendly pre-need statute can alter these numbers. If the law permits me to solicit and retain 20% or more of the revenues generated at the point of the sale, I could conceivably go into the business of a funeral home at a point lower than the above "Rules of Thumb" (*see appendix D*).

Q What is the difference between costs and expenses in view of the budgeting process?

A Expense examples are such things as commissions, overrides and advertising, as opposed to products. Costs in the budgeting process are the acquisition costs of merchandise, such as the wholesale cost of a memorial.

Once the wholesale cost is paid for, a memorial and the price is set, then the expenses incurred to sell that product are added. The result is sales profit or loss before tax. If you saw this as a good question and the answer was helpful, you are in bad need of an *accounting for executives course* at the local university. Run, don't walk.

Q Who is more important in a combination operation, the superintendent of the grounds, the funeral director or the pre-need sales manager?

A Of course, it depends on who you ask. Ask each and you'll hear three different answers. Hopefully, management's position is that the heads of departments are of equal importance to the overall welfare of the corporation. It is well known we can never *convince* a funeral director that he or she would be only equal to a pre-need sales manager or a grounds superintendent. It is critically important, however, that all department heads are viewed by *management* as equals. While the CEO's dealings with department heads may not reflect personal feelings for these people as individuals, the welfare of the firm requires evenhanded treatment.

Q How do I get more referrals from my salespeople?

A As part of the paperwork required to be turned in with a contract, a referral sheet is filled out that identifies the people who
"will be in attendance at the funeral" of this person that's sold.
This would include a list of the pallbearers as they would be
known at the present time. Of course, in cases where you want
to pick up referrals every time, this form would be used before
the presentation begins. If you made a sale, you have names; if
you didn't make a sale, you have the names.

Q Which is most important, a superior salesperson or a superior
lead system?

A I should do more volume with a superior lead system and average salespeople than with superior salespeople and an average
lead system. Superior salespeople are not generally good
prospectors. Therefore, my definition must be that of a closer
rather a superior salesperson. Average salespeople can be taught
to prospect. They will comply, at least until they feel their confidence slipping.

  If we make heritage leads available, they can do well on
those and be more willing to do cold prospecting. The better
they are trained in the referral, the stronger this average person
becomes. They can make their own appointments and learn to
drop by on others. With closers, a lead is an appointment set by
someone else. Interest manifested only by a "tacit approval to
an interview" is not a lead to the strong guy. A superior salesperson will not stay where there is an inferior lead system. By
this, he means appointments.

  Moral to the story is, hire the high quality "person who may
well be a very average salesperson," give him support in the
form of lead sources he can enjoy working, avoid appointment
setting by others and never quit recruiting until the staff is
where you need it. Then recruit some more.

Q What is the most common reason given for salespeople leaving
the sales organization?

A Poor training, poor lead system and the lack of a program where
the prospect is going to lose something if he or she does not act
soon. And the greatest of these is training. If the departing salesperson could be right when he accuses you of weak training,

then that training foundation has to be rebuilt. You have to know he is wrong if you are accused of weak training (You must be absolutely sure your training is what's wrong if something else is wrong).

Q   How do you best handle differences between departments heads?

A   Create a regular meeting schedule of these people, commonly called a "department head meeting," wherein they discuss problems and solutions on an equal basis. When in that room discussing issues, they are known to be equals and none, except for reasons of personality, would be superior to the other.

Q   Are salespeople made or born?

A   They are made. Some, of course, are "born" in the sense that they have a greater propensity toward communication, stubbornness and a drive to achieve. Those people I call "chemists." You can hardly stop them from being effective. But now let's get down to the 95% who are left. These people can be good salespeople after they have been convinced that attributes they possess can be honed and channeled into an effective communication system that resembles *their* best style, not the style of the "hero."

   People who feel good about themselves are teachable. They can be taught the systems and encouraged to find the one that fits their style best. There is an element of stubbornness or "concept orientation" needed in successful sales. There are no more true "wimps" than there are true "heroes." We're now down to 90% of the population. That 90% needs to know that it's possible, and that you have the skills available and will use them in training. Attributes that are marginal can be developed through skills taught.

Q   Are funeral directors professionals, truly?

A   Certainly. Funeral directors, by virtue of training and licensing,are professionals. Actually, there's a conflict. The director has to be a merchandiser, too. Funeral directors are more apt to view themselves as professionals instead of business people. Cemeterians are more apt to view themselves as business people who are *professional* business people. But, there is a conflict since the cemeterian mostly is engaged in the sales business. Both the funeral director and the cemeterian could easily become neurotic. The funeral director is a merchant. He goes to conventions and, again, learns the latest change in how best to arrange merchandise. The cemeterian learns more about business operations at the convention, knowing he has to hurry home and get the sales volume up.

Q At what point should I have a consultant on board for my corporation's activities?

A Certainly for major projects or certainly for major process change. For example, a funeral director entering the cemetery business needs one. A cemeterian going into the vault manufacturing, monument or funeral business needs one. A person hiring key personnel needs one. Consultants are a little bit like lawyers in that you don't use them unless you need them, and then you absolutely use them.

Q How do I pay a consultant?

A Promptly. Then I shall say, ordinarily, consultants work short term on per diem. Typically, consultants do not pay their own expenses. On a long term basis, a retainer arrangement can be achieved much as you would retain an attorney. Consultants then should be paid over a long term a percentage of the new revenues or profits achieved through the areas in which they are affecting the activities of the corporation.

Q How do the duties of a COO differ from those of a CEO?

A A chief operating officer is in charge of all day to day operations of the corporation. The chief executive officer, while performing some specific functions in the organization such as care fund investments, provides board policies to operations and administers same. The CEO is fully responsible (*See Appendix E*).

Q Who should create the budget?

A Each department head should complete his or her own budget. The budgets are then submitted to the controller or chief accountant. The budgets are adjusted by the finance committee and set for the next year. Budgets should be the guidelines; the more important matter is actual performance *against* the budget. Where opportunities exist to undershoot the budget on expenses, for example, that must be done. The next year's budget would then not simply increase last year's budget, but deal with the change in the actual performance.

Q   How frequently should I have a full audit?

A   Time to use your lawyer. Yet, here are some of my thoughts. Every three years. You may, some day, want to sell. Generally, a small corporation does not have any purpose for a complete annual audit. Larger groups, where there are many stockholders, should have a full audit on an annual basis.

Q   If I'm planning a new full service organization (cemetery- funeral home-crematory-mausoleum-lawn crypts) what sequence is optimum?

A   The most important issue facing us is cash flow. You would select the products and services that would provide the maximum cash flow at the outset. The cemetery lot is a given. Fortunately, it is a high cash flow item and our most profitable.

To that, add the right to package in the vault, memorial and the opening and closing. In other words, the customer and the sales advisor negotiate how much of the full package can be handled.

While the mausoleum and garden crypts are great cash cows, they first require short term cash outlay. The laws of the states differ in this regard. Some states allow as many as five years to complete the structure and three years after the first sale before you must start construction. There are fewer dollars both from an inflow and outflow standpoint in the lawn crypt product. High profit. Some short term money going out on the construction is a possibility under some state laws. The product is not well identified in some states which means less regulation regarding time construction and, therefore, cash outflow.

The best of the lot is the funeral home if we confine the discussion to the possibilities of an optimum situation. Short term cash in flow, per case, short term cash out flow (high profits). Guaranteed strong cash flow will depend on a thorough study of the local situation. How much in the first year, the second year? When do I go in the black ? When does the cash flow turn positive? Operationally, the costs of construction of the facilities are in the expenses of operations. At the point of start up, construction and, therefore, cash outlays are heavy in the funeral home and the mausoleum. The monies are borrowed in the ordinary case. Repayment becomes an operational issue. Depreciation is added back in the analysis of the net cash flow.

The other items listed here can create cash in a relative hurry. The at-need funeral cannot. The crematory will feel like a funeral home, in that the in and out flows are short term. While it could produce a profit, the truth is, they generally do not, unless a joint operation has one. Here, the property owner who now is interested in cremation will use the crematory in "his" cemetery. At the same time, the local funeral director will not go to the competitor if he can avoid it. The "long story short" is that crematories are generally not much more than a mama-papa deal unless located in an area where the competition is slim or pricing is without regard to fear. These are not the rule. Paranoia is an emotion. Logic is not. Usually in this circumstance, emotion wins (*See Appendix C*).

Q Who is your firm's "barracuda"?

A First you must know that a barracuda will eat anything in its path. Your firm's barracuda generally resides in a department that has something to do with payroll. This person is almost never enamored by the activities and results in the form of paychecks, of the pre-need sales division, or any sales division. However, barracudas never want to become anything but what they are, so an offer to exchange sharp pencil for a sales kit is forever rejected.

Barracudas, of course, can be found elsewhere other than accounting. Frequently, owners are barracudas. They lure the prey, the sales manager, into the situation and as he becomes effective, they figure out how to eat him up. Barracudas are intelligent; they feel as though once they have seen something work successfully, they can do it themselves. I bet you never knew that sales managers and sales divisions were the favorite food of barracudas.

Q What is wrong with most managers?

A They are not held accountable. Here we write of the managers of the various divisions. Managing funeral director, sales manager, grounds superintendent. Companies that otherwise look good can well be in great trouble if operations managers are left to their own devices. If managers were not provided with a place to sit, such as a desk, but had to move from place to place, they would be much more visible and their workers would feel closer to them, which may in itself be very good or very bad. But, certainly the principle of "walking around management" is a valid principle not adhered to anywhere near enough. Sales managers should be in the field regularly and frequently. "Coach" is a functional term for manager (*See Appendix E*).

Q How much good are psychological tests for personnel?

A The greatest good is they save time. Psychological tests are usually somewhere around 80% accurate. That leaves 20% inaccurate. But, 80% accurate isn't all bad. Usually, after a psychological test has been checked out and gone over with the applicant, the tested individual says, "I knew that all the time." That's probably true, but putting it in this form is new and crystallizes the issues. Of course, the manager has probably saved six months figuring out what style person he's just hired.

Q How do I increase personnel retention?

A An easy answer is to "water their flowers." Our employees, like our children, are subject to a steady dose of critical communications. Or none. Actually, management principles dictate that the job of the manager is to make the life of the employee easier and more effective, just as the job of the employee is to make the manager's life easier and more effective. By easier I don't mean *lazier*. I simply mean more effective. *Management is service.*

Q Who is your firm's "chief hugger"?

A Well, of course, I don't know. But, the question is here because that person rarely hugs people of the same sex. We may have a problem developing here. In these times in particular, the firm is vulnerable to the anger of a disgruntled employee who then takes you to his/her favorite federal or state outlet as he/she attempts to get a pound of flesh. Sexual discrimination can include the hugger. Inappropriate behavior on a corporate level leaves the company and the individual vulnerable.

Q   What is the difference between a $4,000 funeral and a $2,500 funeral?

A   First, about $1,500. Then it must be said the casket is the difference, the services are the same. That over-statement holds up pretty good, but, of course, breaks down in areas of non-service cremations. There are other examples of exceptions, but basically, the price of a funeral is controlled by the price of the casket.

Q   What's happened to direct cremation?

A   I keep praying it's unsatisfying. The first time around in a family, it seems to be a manifestation of the survivors desire to either get rid of the remains fast, or on a higher plane, create their own new standard of the right way to do things. In actual practice, since the funeral's hugging and crying and social dimension have been avoided, direct cremation the second time in the same family is not as likely to happen. As that continues to take place, direct cremation will continue in first time cases and diminish in second time cases, and then lessen, percentage wise, in first time cases.

Q   When will embalming become a law?

A   Never. Certain religions prohibit such a thing.

Q   Why do funerals require a 100% trust deposit in some states and cemetery merchandise trusts requirements are only a fraction of that?

A   Many legislators have difficulty with this one. But then, someone once cautioned me that there are two things a young man should never witness: One is the process of making sausage and the other is the process of making law.

Delivery is the issue. A monument or memorial can be placed on the grave. A vault can be pre-installed. In that activity, an opening and closing has been largely accounted for. A grave space is already there. The effect of the 100% laws is to make more complex the active sale of the funeral on a pre-arranged basis. The creation of 100% laws restricts the funeral director so far as competing with the cemeterian in the joint operation is concerned.

Q   Who sold the first pre-need funeral?

A   Would you believe I do not know. I also do not know who sold the first pre-need cemetery property. Some would point to scriptures for both cases. But, examination shows that Sarah had died in the case of Abram's purchase of the cave of Machpelah and its adjoining land. Ditto for the tomb Christ was buried in, that of Joseph of Arimathia.

In our time, all this cemetery pre-need started post World War II, with the development of the memorial parks by a gent named Doc Williams. The modern funeral sale began, for all intents and purposes, in Dallas, Texas, at the property owned by George Young, *Restland* of Dallas. This was 1954 or 1955.

In the mid-30's, *Forest Lawn* in Glendale, California, established the first funeral home on a cemetery. All this ignores any other possibilities in other countries. I know of none there, but have not researched the issue. I leave that to someone who cares a great deal about playing trivia.

Q   Who started all this "pre-need" stuff in the first place?

A   Actually, funeral directors in the 30's with burial insurance. Cemeteries prior to World War II were primarily community affairs – national, municipal, or non-profit associations. Doing something different and attractive created the memorial park, and that made sense to the public.

The cemeterian then and now knows that if he is not in the pre-need business, he is flirting with bankruptcy (with some isolated exceptions). The funeral director, on the other hand, is delving into the unknown when he goes into pre-need and feels as though he's better off waiting for people to buy at the time of a death. Typically, the cemeterian does not become involved in near as many dollars, contract for contract, as the funeral director does funeral for funeral.

Q   What "can be done" about the escalating high cost of funerals and burials?

A   We are a very capital intensive business. If something were to be done, that's one area in which it should have to be done. Ways will be found to produce smaller funeral homes with less square footage. Since the price of the casket controls the price of the funeral, simplification in the casket could dramatically drop the cost of the funeral. Efforts along these lines will become more and more common as time goes on. The issue is that the high cost cannot effectively be brought down through direct burial and direct cremation. That is never going to work. But simplification of those items requiring high capital expenditures and high merchandise wholesale costs can affect the situation.

Q How do I "get rid of" the "oldtimer" in my company?

A If he is no longer productive or able to increase in his productivity, the subject needs to be dealt with. How it's specifically done is going to have much to do with each operation. But, if you provide the "old timer" with dignity in the maneuver, it can be achieved. Eliminate dignity in the departure process and you may have killed a spirit if not created litigation.

Q What can the public do about higher funeral costs?

A They could do a lot of things, none of which they will do. It has been forever true, they're basically not interested. We see very defensive behavior on a one to one basis. We do, in fact, have an interested public *if* we meet them on the right grounds. Counselors have seen this happen when they find the prospect in the front yard working in the bushes. He lays down his rake and talks, where if we knocked on his door or called him on the phone, he's defensive, somewhat irritated and not anxious to have an interview.

People become very interested when there is a death. They become interested as groups. We have seen high interest at group presentations or at trade shows.

Q How can I help Hospice (or should I)?

A Hospice people should be trained by cemetery and funeral people in specifically "what happens at the time of a death" so that they will know precisely what to do when death takes place. Hospice should be trained to know what pre-arrangement is about and its benefits. I don't see how Hospice can effectively operate without that knowledge.

Q What is the "greatest single attribute" of any employee, from executive to laborer?

A The ability to concentrate. The ability to concentrate buys the fact that that person's life is in reasonable and decent order both at home and on the job. While another person might say integrity, I think integrity is violated in some cases for a long time before anybody knows it. Once the person of integrity has been "caught," integrity built up over a lifetime is destroyed.

Q How should a sales manager treat the counselors he hires?

A He should treat them as he wants them to treat his prospects.

Sales managers frequently hire a counselor after a two or three step interview and then change attitudes toward that person because of non-compliance with something in the system. Once a sales manager has screened an applicant and taken him on board, he must maintain his encouraging posture as he supervises that person. If the sales manager treats his counselor in that fashion, the counselor will treat the customer in that fashion.

Of course, the opposite holds true if the sales manager is mistreating the counselor. The counselor will not treat the prospect in a manner that will gain beneficial results.

Q Should I have an employee handbook?

A Talk to your lawyer about the pitfalls of being too specific in writing. The handbook implies a broad scope of employer rules and regulations and do's and don't's. Management believes ordinarily that a handbook is the most equitable way to be in touch with the employee. In truth, the employee handbook can be used as a weapon against the corporation. Of course, any provision in the handbook not properly worded could end up in the same category. They are not read until someone is preparing to agitate.

Q Should I always interview the spouse of the prospective counselor?

A No. Yet, in a case where the counselor is using his spouses reaction as an excuse, the sales manager ought to make a point of getting together with the spouse. That will at least clarify whether or not that excuse is true, or if that person is using the absent spouse as a stall. Very few spouses (is the plural of spouse, spice?) will be enthusiastic about the counselor working nights on straight commission. While I want to show an interest in the fact that a spouse does exist, I might well want to avoid worrying about interviewing every one of them.

Q   What about trust investments?

A   The issue in the various trusts the cemeterian and funeral director create is growth. The second issue is income. Concentration on growth will, in the long run, produce the needed income. Growth in the portfolio comes from deposits and appreciation. Yet, high income from the trusts is not a bad thing. A high percent of the portfolio in debt instruments produces high income. However, debt instruments do not produce growth. Likely, a percent of the investments in the care fund should be in the likes of bonds and a percent in equities (stocks).

Who knows the right amount? Likely, you do, if an analysis of your needs were to carefully take place, and in the presence of a professional in that field. The Jay Joliat people have a uniquely balanced approach.

Q   What about problems in the mausoleum?

A   Last I knew, the American Cemetery Association study commissioned a few years back is still in print. And is useful. In the indoor units the crypt needs to be drained and vented. The front well sealed. A fellow with problems may well have to go back through and reseal each and every front. Those little flies (gnats) are not against hiding in dark corners and are hard to get. Somewhat like trying to kill dalis grass or onions. Never get it all. Yet, as much as the lot owner complains about weeds on the sections, he may well get more pointed regarding the mausoleum. Your staff needs a licensed spray person. Select one of your people and get him trained. In the long run, this is the best and cheapest way to get the time needed as you tackle this sensitive area. Have you changed your carpet lately?

Q   Does gate income plus investment income equal maintenance costs?

A   Think about that formula. Gate income is defined as interment fees and foundation revenues. First, be convinced there is a need for a goal and the resulting formula. All grounds operations and grounds supervision are to be paid out of the revenues generated from these two sources. Good to have a standard to shoot at on this topic.

Q   Is it oblivion to sell less than you bury?

A   If you now bury more than you sell, you need to give thought to your destiny. Is it not weird to ignore this basic need? Likely – if you have the land – you can use more than this formula indicates. Yet this is the starting place for all operations. T'was certainly that way as each of us began. Wasn't it?

Q   What should the industry do about the funeral/cemetery increasing retail costs?

A   Candy costs more now than before, too. So do a lot of things. In fact, what *has* gone down in price from the price of two or ten years ago? So, why the topic in this material? Simply a caution.

   The public does not care much about our work until the work of an investigative reporter or author sends off a rocket. Then, we hold our breath and ride out the storm and survive. Knowing the attention span of our customers is short, some questions are in order that deal with the right way to think and operate.

   Do I see holding down prices as a public trust or duty? What is my gross and net profit percent goal? Do I have such a thing as a standard that lets me be profitable and hold the line on my prices? Or do I charge as little as possible? Not what the traffic will bear. We are the ultimate in product and service when it comes to vulnerability.

   My point is this. Charging what traffic will bear is not the right thing to do. You need to have a pre-determined profit percentage.

Q   Should I irrigate?

A   Of course I would not irrigate if I did not have to do so. Green does not sell cemetery property in the dry month or six weeks of the typical climate in the United States. In fact, the only two things that sell property are competent salespeople and the grim reaper. If you only want to be greener a few weeks per year than your competitor, abandon that thought and those expenses and give your sod condition the benefit of some of that money. Less weeds. Weed eradication is sorely neglected in the cemetery field. Arid lands require irrigation.

Q   What about the union and the cemetery?

A   Having a union at the establishment is a bit like running two firms. One of which you really do not manage. There are some very beneficial union contracts so far as freedom of operations is concerned. Remember to check the appropriate sections of your union's contract as you undertake new operations.

Q   The non-profit cemetery builds a funeral home, or does it?

A   Yes, it is being done. Carefully, precisely, but it is being done and you, too, can do it. It appears that the overriding issue in this structure is *separateness* of the two operations. Two boards, computer systems, sales efforts, lead systems. Two of everything except the geography and the top person operating the dual complex. It is now another time for me to suggest your employment of your two favorite people. The consultant, since all issues are not legal, and the attorney, since many issues *are* legal.

Q   When it comes to pre-need cremation package selling, is anybody in training?

A   Well, it seems like nobody is in training. I do know that in areas where the cremation percent to the death rate is modest, attention is rarely given to a workman-like approach to the sale of the pre-need cremation package. In fact, little effort is given to diligent follow up of the family after the cremation/funeral to tell of the opportunities for memorialization. Guilty? Hire one person who will have the responsibility to create the organization and the sales in this area. There is plenty of help out there. We don't ignore the topic totally; some of us simply do not organize it, nor do we attempt to direct the effort toward a constant.

Redden's Check list for Cemetery Valuation (generalities)

Higher Valuation*	Lower Valuation
High profit	Low, or no profit
Adequate developed inventory	Low or almost developed
Plenty of undeveloped acreage	Land locked
High yield per acre	Space sales only
High percent mausoleum, G/C & L/C	Single depth and height
Overhead costs in control	High (casual) cost approaches
High sales volume & adequate mark up	Inability to sell weak price policy
Keeps paper (and interest)	Banks paper, loses interest
Plenty of receivables	Low volume of accounts
Good quality receivables	Receivables not monitored
Plenty cash and reserves invested	Low cash, reserves not invested
Inventory of paid merchandise	No or low paid inventory
Plenty of modern equipment	Short on modern equipment
High value buildings	Low value buildings
Paved roads	Roads in poor condition
Trusts aggressively invested	Income position, almost exclusively
Long term people, trained	High turnover – too new
Future deliveries funded	Unfunded, uninstalled, merchandise
Strong at need sales	Weak at need sales

(*stolen from Mr. Anonymous and revised*)

Q   What is Redden's chronology for placing a funeral home on a cemetery?

A   First, hire the most experienced consultant available for guidance, analysis and pro forma. General scheduling benchmarks should include:

Month one	Zoning
	Legal issues regarding marketing and selling
	Legal, general
	Select architect
	Arrange financing
	Hire a Funeral Director
	Appoint a Sales Director
Month three	Prepare and finalize bids
	Finalize software
Month four	Begin construction
Month six	Begin personnel cross training
	Begin public relations work, company newsletter, letters to groups
Month ten	Begin advertising campaign
Month eleven	End construction
Month twelve	Open for business

Q   Will a mortuary on a cemetery plateau at 75% of interments?

A   When we consider the pre-need funeral sales at combination firms is less than 40 years old and that there are still a small minority of combination firms, the 75% figure is still out for research. Yet, it is the case that to date this is the figure the new combination may well look to. There is a need to establish the specific figures for this specific project.

   The first year may, like the last, be a figure other than what you had heard. If the population of my area reveals 50% destined to use another establishment for reasons of race and/or religion, the total population you are dealing with is reduced or amended by a predictable percent. Now, figure the pro forma again (*See Appendix D*).

Q   Ninety Five percent of the funerals your combo handles go where?

A Again, the evidence to date is strong that the funerals held at your combination will stay in your cemetery. The public thinks it is a lot owners' cemetery. Don't waste advertising dollars trying to undo this.

Q What is the cost of establishing a sales force?

A In the first three months, $20,000 should cover the budget. Here, we are hiring a new Sales Director and starting the acquisition of a sales force. This scenario holds the hiring of a Sales Director with sales management skills, but not cemetery skills. He will learn the product.

After that point, the normal budget kicks in. The sales expenses shall be budgeted at 35% of revenue generated in the cemetery sale and 12% in the funeral pre-need sales, plus or minus two points due to the age and health factors of the pre-need customer. There are a few experienced combination Sales Directors with a track record. Many of those few are too "pricey." Hire a professional manager and teach him the products and services.

Q How many pre-need cemetery packages will one salesperson sell in a month?

A The answer is six. Count on this as you figure out how many people it will take to produce the revenue needed to meet your goals.

Q How many funeral pre-need sales account for one death?

A The best we can calculate at present is that 50 pre-need contracts will produce one at need case in the following 30 days. This statistic serves as a way for us to aid in the projection of the at-need case load, since the pre-need is converted to an at-need at the death. If I sold 100 pre-need contracts in a month, I should look for two of them to become at-need. Do not make your projections cumulative. Simply use this figure, one month at a time, as you project case load from the pre-need effort. Then target the situation.

Q Should I advance commissions?

A   Pay front money. To advance is to be vulnerable. It is to issue a license for larceny. As careful as you may be in hiring and screening, you tempt the system by advancing. Insurance companies advance on the pre-need funeral sale, and I am glad to get it. The reason they do it is that they have to. As the field matures, the insurance companies will do what they want to do instead of what they have to do. When they advance to you, they are, in one way or the other, charging for the use of that money. How much and in what form, I do not know. Truth is, no one gives money away.

Q   How much cash should pre-need sales bring in?

A   A minimum of 20% in down payments should come in with your contracts. Obviously, if that happened on each contract, the issue of advance would not be an issue. The 20% is an average to look for over a month's period.

Q   Should I sue bad accounts?

A   Sure. Never disappoint your customer. He expects you to try to collect the debt. So, do that, including sue for the debt.

Q   Should I charge interest, how much and what system?

A   Yes again; he expects to pay for the use of money. I suggest a look at the use of add-on as the vehicle of choice. It is easy to figure and sounds a whole lot better as you talk. As you fill out the contract, finish the clarification of the APR.

Q   Why hold back opening/closing in the pre-need sale?

A   The vast majority of the operations still do not sell the opening/closing. Better I have the money to invest at compounded rates or, better yet, in equities, at least in part, than the customer. He will gladly turn the opening/closing money over to you.

    Inflation at any rate will lag far behind interest compounded, since money is, after all, a commodity for sale and sets the pace for all else. Pay commission on that sale by first charging an "inflation factor of three or four years." Then, trust deposit all the balance of the proceeds of that sale. Coordinate that sale with the package you need to sell at this point in time at your property.

Q   Should you hire female grounds employees?

A   I have no experience directly with this idea. I do know of operations who have token women on the grounds force. I know of no operation that attempts to provide equal balance with male grounds employees. The problems of separate facilities and possible distractions may add to the scarcity. How about an all women force?

Q   Do funeral directors do well at learning grounds operations at the combination?

A   Not in my experience. They generally have no time for the other areas outside of the funeral operations. See Appendix A for a suggested list of early interests for a funeral director to look to in the event he/she was hired before the combinations funeral home was open. He/she will never get it done.

Q   Well then, where can this change?

A   The curriculum at the embalming school is the likely place. At present, little is taught at the school regarding cemeteries. The funeral director will leap out in front of the race for better people in the joint operations when his schooling adds the cemetery to the studies. This should be done. The cemetery people have nothing even approaching the schooling the funeral director receives as he prepares to be a licensed professional.

Q   Shall we have sod or weeds?

A   Few cemeteries have agronomists or horticulturalists as superintendents. I personally had the pleasure of working with them for a number of years. You would think these people would be the first on board. If I had a budget that let me either fertilize grass or kill weeds, I would likely kill the weeds. Of course, in Bermuda country, killing the grass is next to impossible and weeds come in many varieties. Get professional help, or contract out that portion of the rounds operations, or call your county agent.

Q   Is it time for a real university?

A   American Cemetery Association take note. Why don't you buy an operation in a community of 500,000 or more people. It would be a cemetery. We then staff the cemetery university with dues-paying students. Soon, we build the mortuary and staff same with students wanting to learn the combination business from the funeral directing viewpoint. All are for profit. The faculty is made up of academically qualified people in the cemetery and funeral fields. We get certified. We operate at a profit. A hands on school. Hurry up and do it so I can be the first President of the ACA University.

Q   Who should the salespeople think they are?

A   To tell the truth, I believe they should think they are advisers. Counseling is not a strong enough word for what we should be doing. "My advise to you folks is to get this done now." I think even the author could teach an otherwise marginal, or worse, salesperson who is afraid of high pressure selling, to give advice. (With the help of his wife).

Q   Do you have a rule of thumb for management's attitude?

A   Rule of thumb: Your people want to do the right thing.

This truth is mindful of the fact that we as a nation are always one generation away from great improvements in human relations. Our children start out as reaching, groping infants. Somehow, we adults repeat errors of history, and troubles come about as certain as the hope is there that we will do otherwise.

Delegate	Encourage
Show interest	Coach
Inform	Discipline
Ask opinions	Show humor
Give credit	Be available

The personnel file of each employee should include any special skills. By doing that, we found a stone setter. You might find a tree person, an electrician, a jack of all trades, a computer person or an entertainer for your annual get-together. As the employee tells you of the special skills possessed, pride in that skill shows. That is not all bad.

Q   What are commissions for the funeral pre-need sale?

A   We must assume the establishment is in a state that permits funds to be used for costs, including commissions. Many of the firms are using insurance as the vehicle of choice for reasons including the fact that the proceeds are tax exempt (still true). Another reason is the availability of any funds at all with which to pay commissions. In 100% law states, the pre-need funeral can hardly be solicited since there are no funds with which to pay people to solicit the sale.

How much commission to pay is the question. First, decide on how much the firm should realize on each sale for each category of age and health issues. Carriers differ here. Then, factor in 1.5%, plus or minus, for the sales coaching needed and the rest is available for the compensation of the salesperson. Much less is paid per agreement than the typical 15% paid to a cemetery salesperson. In the funeral, it may average a range of three to nine percent of face amount, depending on ages and health. People can make a good living at those rates since the sale is larger than the usual cemetery sales and the frequency of finding someone willing to talk about the topic is greater than is the case in the cemetery sale.

Q   True or false, the funeral price delivered by a combination firm is lower in price to the public than for the free-standing, independent funeral?

A   False. Logic has it that the costs are, by definition, lower in the combination. This is only logical. Not empirical. One can find many ways to waste people and funds and still be in the combination business. That having been said, where the same person in the combination is regularly used for task performance in the funeral operations and the cemetery operations, there will be services delivered at lower costs. For example, a firm owning a combination establishment and a free standing funeral home will have lower costs in the combination, given fairness in allocating costs. Whether the lower costs are passed on to the public is another matter.

Q   Why do sales organizations, staffed with competent people, fail?

A   Reasons for the public to "buy now," are called programs. If the prospect can put off the purchase indefinitely and not suffer loss beyond the inflation factor, the organization is crippled. Gimmicks or schemes are unhappy words in our work, but they are the words used to describe the needed element - an imperative. Buy "now" or lose. A dress sale, a suit sale and a short term rebate in a car dealership all provide reasons to act or lose. Others call them sales rebates, etc. We call them programs.

We need programs, since the public does not want what we have and since that will not change. Examples of programs are a discount limited on some basis, two for one, free space, payment moratorium, balance forgiven in event of a death, interest free periods, etc. Features that are built in are the credit exchange plan and child protection.

Other reasons for failure are to be found. Not working may well do it. Since we started this question with the premise that we had competent people, we must be stretching competence to include hard work. Know any competent people that are lazy, or lazy people that are competent?

Q   What rating tool should be used as you interview?

A   As you sit across the desk from the candidate, pay attention to the following and rate the person, in each category, after he/she leaves. Use the numbers one through five, with five being the best. If the totals do not exceed 25, resist the temptation to hire. Your instincts are being endorsed by specific judgements in the areas indicated by the words. I adapted this years ago from an American Cemetery Association sales management workbook, edited by Frank Karnes, past president of The American Cemetery Association. It is changed some from what he wrote, but who ever said Frank was perfect?

Verbal Facility   Resilient
Word choice   Open Personality
Thick Skinned   Friendly
Stubborn   Listener
Appearance   Inter-Personal Skills
(See Appendix F)

Q   What is an *extended family service counselor?*

A   I swiped this one from Dan Reed, past president of The American Cemetery Association. Rather than having two sales forces, there is one. All can qualify for "duty" by virtue of production and proper behavior. This system keeps the competition at a high level. While the term was Dan's, I have used this system for many, many years as CEO of this place or that. The point is to not permit brutes to handle families that come in to make arrangements at the time of a death.

Q   Which is the fastest way to the bottom line, sales increase or expense reduction?

A   Again, if you see this as a really good question, don't tell anyone. Run to the nearest adult class on business issues, most particularly those that have to do with *finances*.

Anyway, lets pretend you need to come up with $30,000 in some measured period of time. If net profit before tax is 30%, you will have to generate $100,000 in new sales to gain the $30,000. On the other hand, a $30,000 reduction in expenses goes straight to the bottom line (like alcohol rushes to the blood stream). Complicating the sales approach is the flow of the cash and the cancellation rate. On the other hand, sales are "more likely" than expense reduction if you have been running a tight ship. And on the third hand, if that were true, why do you need this extra money anyway?

Q   What about public relations?

A   "Nothing new under the sun," says the writer of Ecclesiastes. Our public is both obvious and subtle. Be sure to identify them.

1. Your employees
2. The general public
3. The clergy
4. The Legislator
5. Suppliers
6. Immediate family
7. Location neighbors
8. Competition
9. And the last shall be first, the lot owner, and/or, the families you have served through the funeral home.

Public relations is the concern of all. Each of us is or is not cordial in behavior and in what is said. Publish a newsletter to the "public." All but the general public can be on the list. It is good business to do this.

Q   What are the qualities of good supervisors?

A   In 1962, G. J. Klupar, Administrator of the Catholic cemeteries of the Archdiocese of Chicago, wrote a definitive book, *Modern Cemetery Management*. Nothing like it since, until, on the subject of funeral homes, Howard C. Rather edited the N.F.D.A's resource manual in 1984. Each of us should have copies of both works.

From Klupar's book, his thoughts on supervisors: "Good basic intelligence, unquestioned loyalty, ability to work well with others and command respect, a fine sense of distinction between the important and the unimportant, effective organization in planning work, superior judgement in all circumstances, effective communication and practical knowledge of cemetery administration. Industry and a capacity to give unselfishly also are essential." Almost all of that applies to good fathers and husbands. Fathers and husbands usually do not have to have a practical knowledge of cemeteries.

Q   When is a business plan needed?

A   Starting a new business requires a study of the market place as regards to our product. The same is true of the acquisition. Who in the area is now supplying what we are going after and what is the loyalty of the public to the suppliers? An acquisition requiring capital will need to show the lender how many dollars are needed and a clear plan as to how and over what period of time the lender will get his money back at a profit. If the subject is an acquisition of a cemetery by a funeral home, *careful* is the word. Cemeteries are long term businesses, replete with contingent liabilities. By comparison, the funeral home deals in short term cash flow. What percent of the population already owns lots locally and in their own name? Would they change cemeteries? Likely not. Has the cemetery sold merchandise and services pre-need in the past and have the funds needed to supply the products and services been set aside in a fashion that will cover costs? What are the laws on the cemetery business? If a funeral home is to go on a cemetery, the usual questions that need to be posed through the business plan, and answered, are supplemented by the issue of the location of the establishment. That funeral home on that cemetery is for those lot owners. Are there enough of them at the local death rate to support a funeral home if 75% of the interments were the most funerals that could be achieved?

A fifteen page business plan is needed to cover those issues and others. It is a short document, done by professionals. Short, because the lender will not take the time to read and become interested in the business. In the first section of the plan, he must see the answers to the money questions. Get help on this (*See Appendix D*).

Q What about conglomerates?

A If futures in the business are important, then we must applaud the entry on the scene of the "conglomerates." The cemetery business as it now operates, is only a baby. The movement is as recent as post World War II. It started with aggressive marketing and sales. That movement and the resulting popularity of the pre-need purchase has made the purpose of the conglomerates possible and profitable. The funeral service professional, until the pre-need issues and the resulting growth of acquisitions, was operating on today's level, but in much the same manner as it had for generations.

Thirty years after the birth of the conglomerate, the vast majority of cemeteries and funeral homes are "mama-papa" businesses. I cannot imagine that this will change to the extent consolidation has taken place in the areas of retail. So, we have the best of both worlds. Futures for both the personnel and the businesses. Now the same owner might well find a ready market for his business, should he desire to do so. Individuals have an opportunity to grow in the merged and acquired firms, past and future.

Q What are the physical and emotional characteristics of people that purchase mausoleum crypts. How do they differ from ground site purchases?

A They all look the same to me. If I build a 1000 crypt unit, I may have 50 of them taken from me. I will have to sell the rest. These 50 units represent 25 couples that likely don't like something about the ground. These people are usually nice folks, but otherwise are equipped equally with those I have to sell. The moral is, don't build a building for the 2.5%. The rest will break your little heart.

Q What is the secret business plan?

A   Going into a "deal" requires we know the overall goal, how and when we will arrive there and the costs and rewards. Those issues are not secret. Usually missing is a detailed plan on getting out should something go radically wrong. The secret plan is the parachute. How do I bail out? What are the likely costs and when is the proper timing? Define the circumstances that would bring about such a move. What if the joint-ventured funeral home and cemetery does not work out due to the sovereignty issue? Be ready with a buy-sell agreement in that event, just as you would have one in the event of a death of a partner.

Always strap on the parachute. Even when you are certain you will never use it.

Ten Thoughts Regarding the Interment Process.

The interment site is the "show place" for the degree of your concern for the family interring a loved one. Too often in our routines, we forget this fact. We have funerals every day; the family does not.

1. An idea for leading funerals. Use arrows with numbers on them. Or, arrows, each of a different color. This saves man hours for the superintendent, freeing him to police the area of the interment. This saves embarrassment where one is not apt to keep his vehicles in tip-top shape.

2. Grounds people could be of great help while waiting for a service to come in. Wisk brooms to sweep off nearby memorials and the grass at the interment site. Weed pulling in nearby flower beds, cloths to polish tent poles, pick up papers and other debris lying around nearby.

3. Clean chair covers. People notice a mess. Even when their own homes are in a mess. There is no excuse for unsightly equipment at the interment, but reasons abound. The management never checks. The CEO never walks the grounds. He delegates absolutely everything.

4. Provide tent heaters for cold weather. Provide lap blankets. Thoughtful, yes. Evidence of your awareness of their situation, yes.

5. No dirt mounds. They are a crass reminder of the next location of that dirt. Charge extra for the extra effort to remove all dirt from the site, but do it.

6. Have tents on wheels, or provide a system in which the tents are not taken down and put up for each interment. If you have tents not on wheels, rig a system whereby the backhoe is used to transport the tents. An interment chapel may be appropriate.

7. As the superintendent checks the interment site, he should have "survey flags" to use in marking sites that need the attention of the maintenance people. I first saw these in use at *Englewood Park Cemetery* when Kermit Johnson was the general manager. Later, I have seen them at *Fairmount Cemetery* in Denver, Colorado. Frank Hegner has the flags printed with a message telling the lot owners that special work is about to take place at their sites. Different colors for different jobs. Blue for memorial work, red for sunk graves, etc.

8. Have your people in uniforms. Never permit shirtless personnel.

9. Most funeral directors are well aware the cemetery is responsible for what happens at the cemetery during the interment service. The stress comes about when the cemetery is not sharp in their concern for family welfare at the site. The funeral director can get antsy and act as though he is in charge at the interment location. His responsibility is not dropped as the procession enters the grounds. The interment operation ends the service. Let it be done in a manner that is edifying to the family. The cemetery's long term relationship with the lot owner now begins.

    Lay the flowers down. Tossing them is not acceptable. Have a pre-set arrangement, a pattern for the placement. Finish the work. Never leave the grave incomplete. In appropriate seasons, get the sod down and tamped. Finish your work. In seasons where the earth is frozen, get all done that is humanly possible.

10. Mowing and snow removal are both issues regarding the interment site. Even in times when the grass is getting ahead of the workers, have that site cleaned and ready. In wet and/or slippery weather, place mats from the roadside to the tent.

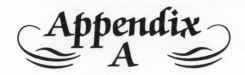

Appendix A

QUESTIONNAIRE

This quiz should be given to any person in the firm that must have a general knowledge of the entire operations. Make your adjustments to the questions as applicable. In any case, never permit a Family Service Adviser to go on duty until he/she can fill out 80% of the answers correctly. At that point, the manager of that person should give an oral quiz on the topics. Two hours will be needed.

1. The proper word for burial: _____

2. The word used in describing the placement of casketed remains in a mausoleum crypt: _____

3. A permanent bronze cube for remains: _____

4. If a couple owns four spaces, #1-2-3-4, and the man dies and the wife chooses number 2 for his burial, which space would be used at the time of her death? _____

5. In a side by side mausoleum crypt entombment, is the man placed on the right or left? _____

6. What information can be found on an interment card?

   _____

7. If the map is unclear as to whether burial has taken place or not, where would you check for a burial? _____

8. What rights does the Certificate of Ownership give to the owner? _____

9. Where would you find the original sales contract? _____

   _____

10. What two things are required before a cremation?_____

    _____

11. Is a receipt required at the time cremated remains are picked up? _____

12. Who should sign the interment authorization? _____

13. When would the above not be applicable? _____

14. Who should sign the cremation authorization? _____

15. Who issues permits to cremate? _____

16. Should a person put the wishes to be cremated in a will? Why?
    _____

17. A vault/section crypt is required under law by the state, yes or no. If yes, why? _____

18. What is a lawn crypt and how many spaces would be needed for burial of five people? _____

19. What is a niche? _____

20. What is columbarium? _____

21. Who signs the Certificate of Ownership? _____

22. Do we bill out of town funeral homes for cremations and interment fees? _____

23. Who can purchase property? _____

24. All burials in the park are completed with the feet facing East?
    ❏ True ❏ False

25. If a burial should be completed in the wrong space, what must be done to correct this? _____

26. Is the interment charge for a service at 3:45 p.m. on Monday the same as 8:30 a.m. on Saturday? Yes____No_____. Is it the same for 1:30 p.m. on Sunday? Yes____No_____.

27. Who quotes the charge for a "direct" cremation? _____

28. Is the charge for a cremation the same as an interment fee?
    Yes____No_____.

29. What can we do about having the family sign the interment authorization if the family is out of town and will not be here until the day of the service? _____
    _____

30. There are no sections in the cemetery used for single burial only? ❏ True ❏ False

31. If you have a family who wants to change locations, what is the proper procedure? _____
    _____

32. A name change should always be done on an at-need situation when property is being given by someone else? ❏ True ❏ False

33. The cemetery will always repurchase property from a lot owner for the current day prices? ❏ True ❏ False

34. When doing a location change or name change we do not need the deed if the property is only changing within the family?
    ❏ True ❏ False

35. When a funeral home calls about an interment, you do not need to pull any records except the lot owner's card?
☐ True ☐ False

36. If the lots are listed in the husband's name only, upon his death, provided there is no will, who has rights to the property?

_____

37. Cemetery property is considered real estate property for taxes?
☐ True ☐ False

38. What is an inscription blank and when should it be completed?

_____

When completed, who gets the information? _____

39. How can you find the owner of the property when you have only the location? _____

40. At the time of death, anyone can order a marker for the deceased? ☐ True ☐ False

41. When the memorial has been ordered, it will take approximately two weeks for delivery? ☐ True ☐ False

42. We cannot match the very old markers in the cemetery, only the ones sold after 1955? ☐ True ☐ False

43. When you put on a contract that you want an exact match, you can change the marker from a 24" x 12" to a 24" x 14"so that the match can have a vase? ☐ True ☐ False

44. We only sell one type of vase, true or false? ☐ True ☐ False

45. You can have a single marker on the top of the grave and a government marker on the foot of the grave? ☐ True ☐ False

46. If the husband has a government marker, then the wife cannot have a marker to match? ☐ True ☐ False

47. The charge for the government marker is to cover the shipping and handling from the factory? ☐ True ☐ False

48. *Rockedge* is the description of the granite border on the marker base? ☐ True ☐ False

49. All the granite used under the markers in the park is pink with a four inch border? ☐ True ☐ False

50. How many letters will fit on a single marker? _____

51. Does the design change when the size changes? _____

52. What is the purpose of the marker acknowledgement card?

_____

53. The TOGETHER FOREVER emblem is automatically ordered as part of the marker design shown on the sample in the display room? ☐ True ☐ False

54. Can a 16" x 8" baby marker be used anywhere in the park? ____
55. What information is needed for the scroll on a companion marker for the living spouse? _____
56. There is no additional charge for a scroll? ❑ True ❑ False
57. You cannot use full dates (month, day, year) on a scroll?
    ❑ True ❑ False
58. What do you do when the size is not shown on the interment card and you want an exact match? _____
59. Is there an additional charge for any emblem used on a marker?
    _____
60. When would there be an additional charge? _____
61. Can you have a photograph put on a marker? _____
62. Do we charge for emblems used in the mausoleum? If yes, how much? _____
63. Do any organizations provide emblems? _____
64. Are there niches in the garden mausoleum? _____
65. Do we scatter ashes? ❑ Yes ❑ No. Do we have a plaque?
    ❑ Yes ❑ No. If we do have a plaque, where is it located?
    _____
66. When a family comes into the office to pay on an account, what information should you get from them? _____
67. The contract is always listed in the name of the deceased?
    ❑ True ❑ False
68. Where do you go to find out if a pre-need vault has been installed? _____
69. If a family has a large "cash" down-payment, what should you do with the money? _____
70. When you have a name change, you should notify only accounting? ❑ True ❑ False
71. When should the name and address be legible on a contract?
    _____
72. If a family does not pay their bill, we never sue or go to court to collect? ❑ True ❑ False
73. When a family comes into the office with a statement from the bank, who should talk with them? _____
74. If a family has questions regarding their funeral bill, who should help them? _____
75. When the contract is cancelled, we refund all the money to the family? ❑ True ❑ False
76. Equity is good forever? ❑ True ❑ False

77. The cemetery will not file in probate court for a claim, the family must do that themselves? ❑ True ❑ False

78. There is no charge for transferring property? ❑ True ❑ False

79. When arranging a disinterment, only the property owner has to sign the disinterment papers? ❑ True ❑ False

80. There is no other paperwork necessary for a disinterment? ❑ True ❑ False

81. All disinterments will be done at the time best for the family and they may be present at the time of removal? ❑ True ❑ False

82. Family members are encouraged to stay for the interment after a service also? ❑ True ❑ False

83. When you want spaces put on hold or marked sold, you should mark the maps and ledgers in pencil yourself? ❑ True ❑ False

84. There is no charge for putting spaces on hold? ❑ True ❑ False

85. Spaces will be held for 30 days? ❑ True ❑ False

86. If wrong information is found on the original contract, interment card or lot owner's card, you should change it? ❑ True ❑ False

87. You should always file back all cards in the vault yourself? ❑ True ❑ False

88. When you are going to make a pre-need presentation, you can take any information from the vault and return it the next day, such as interment cards etc? ❑ True ❑ False

89. We have burials in the park 365 days a year? ❑ True ❑ False

90. Our funeral home cannot handle a service unless the body has been embalmed? ❑ True ❑ False

91. Who completes the Death Certificate? _____

92. The last funeral home to handle the body does all the paperwork on a ship-in? ❑ True ❑ False

93. Because of the religious differences, we cannot handle a Jewish service? ❑ True ❑ False

94. You must have a clergyman handle a chapel service? ❑ True ❑ False

95. All caskets must have a pall or covering? ❑ True ❑ False

96. An American flag can be used by a veteran, but there is an additional cost for the flag? ❑ True ❑ False

97. No artificial flowers can be used in a funeral service? ❑ True ❑ False

98. Casket palls are always made of flowers? ❑ True ❑ False

99. When you are unable to locate an exact grave space, you should guess before you bother any of the supervisors or superintendents? ❑ True ❑ False

100. You can always rely on the maps in the vault when trying to find a space to sell? ❑ True ❑ False

101. Artificial flowers are always allowed in approved vases? ❑ True ❑ False

102. We allow only fresh flowers in the mausoleum and the family must place them? ❑ True ❑ False

103. You can have only one arrangement of flowers per grave, except on special holidays? ❑ True ❑ False

104. You need to check an at-need lot sale when you have more than one space; single spaces sold at-need do not need verification? ❑ True ❑ False

105. Who acts for the corporation if top management is unavailable and a corporation decision must be decided? _____

106. Distinerments do not have to be approved before they can be processed? ❑ True ❑ False

107. In what event(s) would management disqualify a counselor from standing duty? _____

108. What do you do if a customer wants to transfer lots in at-need situations? _____
    In pre-need situations? _____

109. How do you find information about when a marker is due or ordered on a weekday? _____
    On a weekend? _____

110. There is a current price book kept under the front counter for anyone who needs to use it at anytime? ❑ True ❑ False

111. A potted plant can be placed on a grave anytime during the year? ❑ True ❑ False

112. We can always obtain any flowers wanted by a family? ❑ True ❑ False

113. Where are (a) Lot owner's file: _____
    (b) Interment file: _____
    (c) Ledger books: _____
    (d) Interment journals: _____

114. Do we keep a count of the number of interments in the park? If yes, how? _____

115. Can a counselor take a map out of the office to help find a location? _____

116. The ladies in the front office are supervised by whom?
_____

117. Counselors, who is your "Boss" when you are on duty?
_____

118. _____ primary job is? _____
     (Person's Name)

119. _____primary job is? _____
     (Person's Name)

120. _____primary job is? _____
     (Person's Name)

121. _____primary job is? _____
     (Person's Name)

122. _____ is in charge of the Accounting Department?

123. The cemetery was founded when? _____

124. The mausoleum was built when? _____

125. The funeral home was opened when? _____

126. In what section was the first interment made and in what year?
_____

127. Who are the officers of the company? List their names and their
     positions with the corporation: _____
_____

128. Who are the members of the Board of Directors? _____
_____

129. List the major divisions of the company and the manger of
     each. _____
_____

Appendix B

Sales Organization Check List
Structure

1. **Sales Manager**
   A. Are his responsibilities written down?
   B. Has he signed off on them?
   C. Does he have input into pricing?
   D. Does he have input into policy and programs?
   E. Does he have the right to sell?
   F. What is his compensation system?
   G. How long has he been on the job?
   H. Who does he report to?
   I. Who in the organization is his equal?
   J. Does he meet on a regular basis with other department heads?
   K. Is he a good recruiter?
   L. What is his budget?
   M. Does he have a part in budget preparation?
   N. Does he have a field responsibility?
   O. Does he operate solely as an administrator?
   P. If he does not go into the field, what is the reason?
   Q. Does he have incentive dollars available?
   R. How often does he hold sales meetings and how long are they?
   S. Is he an effective sales person in his own right?
   T. Is he a good detail person?
   U. Is he honest?
   V. Can you trust him?
   W. Is he a relative of ownership or top management?
   X. What is his report system (how are salespeople held accountable)?

2. Top Management

A. Do you resent the sales director's income?

B. Who is the corporate barracuda (and why is he/she effective)?

C. What products and services do you permit to be sold pre-need?

D. Do the salespeople serve on the at-need level?

E. What is the commission structure?

F. Outline the "program" the public is offered (ex.ample, free space).

G. What is the sales budget process?

H. How often and with what notice are price increases made?

I. Do you like salespeople?

J. Have you ever been "taken" by salespeople?

K. Do you have a separate family service division?

L. Do the pre-need people have access to the post interment lead?

M. What are the trust laws for the merchandise, funeral and care fund?

N. What is the ratio of mausoleum sales to overall volume?

O. What is the ratio of memorial sales to overall volume?

P. What is the ratio of pre-need funeral volume to overall volume?

Q. What is the annual interment count?

R. What is the total number of interments?

S. When was your funeral home established?

T. Do any of your family actively work in the day-to-day operations?

U. What is the sales volume history of pre-need and at-need?

V. Are you impetuous (known for frequent change, without notice)?

W. Do you sell trusts and insurance?

X. Who are your independent contractor and who are employees?

3. **Salespeople**

   A. How many?

   B. How many with you over a year?

   C. What is the average volume per counselor?

   D. What is their standard presentation?

   E. What is the standard kit?

   F. What reporting do they do and to whom?

   G. What percent of the pre-need business is written after 6:00 p.m.?

   H. What percent of business is written on Saturday or Sunday?

   I. What is the primary lead source?

   J. What is your usual volume?

   K. How much money do you make per month?

   L. Is the Sales Director well trained?

   M. Do you receive a salary?

   N. Are your commissions advanced?

   O. What is your strong point in selling skills?

   P. What is your weak point?

   Q. How did you get into the business?

   R. What is your education level?

   S. Do you have another source of income?

   T. Are you married, separated, divorced, widowed? Do you have any children? What are their ages and sex?

   U. Are you well trained?

   V. Do you do any reading on sales, attend professional groups?

   W. Do you have good sales meetings?

   X. What would you change about the company that would increase your income?

   Y. Is the company trustworthy?

   Z. What is your numbers awareness? Are you prompt and accurate on reports? Do you set goals and keep aware of them?

Appendix C

GENERIC

STEPS TO PROFIT PRE-NEED SALES PROGRAMS

	Full TPA *		Lots Only		Pre-Need Marker		Vault-Marker		Lawn Crypt		Garden Crypts		Mausoleum	
Average selling price	100%	$1,910.00	100%	$700.00	100%	$500.00	100%	$950.00	100%	$1,200.00	100%	$1,500.00	100%	$2,300.00
Cost of Land		$5.00		$5.00		-0-		-0-		$2.50		$1.00		$1.66
Architect, construction, merchandise	21%	$408.00			45%	$227.00	36%	$346.00	27%	$323.00	27%	$405.00	20%	$450.00
Sales costs: Total Commission Plus sales mgmt. Plus advertising Plus pres. kits	35%	$669.00	25%	$175.00	25%	$125.00	25%	$238.00	31%	$272.00	31%	$465.00	31%	$713.00
Perpetual Care	7% (L)	$140.00	20%	$140.00		-0-		-0-	6% (L)	$70.00	10%	$150.00	10%	$230.00
Overhead	5%	$96.00	5%	$35.00	5%	$25.00	5%	$48.00	5%	$60.00	5%	$75.00	5%	$115.00
Loan Costs (Based on 12% of construction cost)		-0-		-0-		-0-		-0-		-0-		$21.00		-0-
Gross profit	31%	$592.00	50%	$345.00	25%	$123.00	34%	$318.00	34%	$373.00	25%	$375.00	34%	$790.00

* TPA means Total Prearrangement; Property, Memorial, Internment and vault.

Appendix C — continued

STEPS TO PROFIT PRE-NEED SALES PROGRAMS

	Full TPA *		Lots Only		Pre-Need Marker		Vault-Marker		Lawn Crypt		Garden Crypts		Mausoleum	
Dollars Retained Cemetery Profit Plus Care	38%	$732.00	70%	$485.00	25%	$123.00	34%	$318.00	37%	$443.00	35%	$525.00	44%	$1,020.00
Interest Income (60% of Interest Receivable)	10%	$191.00	5%	$35.00	5%	$25.00	5%	$48.00	5%	$60.00	5%	$75.00	10%	$230.00
Total To Cemetery Profit Plus Perpetual Care Plus Interest	48%	$923.00	75%	$520.00	30%	$148.00	39%	$366.00	42%	$503.00	40%	$600.00	54%	$1,250.00
Profit Plus Interest Only	41%	$783.00	55%	$380.00	30%	$148.00	38%	$366.00	36%	$433.00	30%	$450.00	44%	$1,020.00
Merchandise Trust Return		$82.00		-0-		$45.00		$69.00		$50.00		-0-		-0-
Profit Plus Interest Plus Merchandise Trust Return	45%	$865.00	55%	$380.00	39%	$193.00	46%	$483.00	40%	$483.00	30%	$450.00	44%	$1,020.00

* TPA means Total Prearrangement; Property, Memorial, Internment and vault.

Funeral Home – Cemetery On-Site Combination

Generic Projections for Year 1
For purpose of usable percents

	Month #1	Month #2	Month #3	Month #4	Month #5	Month #6	Month #7
MARKET SHARE INTERMENTS	29	29	29	29	29	29	29
# OF FUNERAL SERVICES	3	3	4	4	4	4	4
% OF MARKET SHARE	10.3%	10.3%	13.8%	13.8%	13.8%	13.8%	13.8%
CASKET & SERVICES	4,500.00	4,500.00	4,500.00	4,500.00	4,500.00	4,500.00	4,500.00
REVENUE:							
FUNERAL CHARGES	6,750.00	6,750.00	9,000.00	9,000.00	9,000.00	9,000.00	9,000.00
CASKET	6,750.00	6,750.00	9,000.00	9,000.00	9,000.00	9,000.00	9,000.00
VAULTS	2,100.00	2,100.00	2,800.00	2,800.00	2,800.00	2,800.00	2,800.00
CLOTHING, CARDS, ETC.	405.00	405.00	540.00	540.00	540.00	540.00	540.00
	16,005.00	16,005.00	21,340.00	21,340.00	21,340.00	21,340.00	21,340.00
COSTS PER SERVICE:							
CASKET COSTS	2,126.25	2,126.25	2,835.00	2,835.00	2,835.00	2,835.00	2,835.00
VAULT COSTS	841.05	841.05	1,121.40	1,121.40	1,121.40	1,121.40	1,121.40
MISC. COSTS	143.34	143.34	191.12	191.12	191.12	191.12	191.12
	3,110.64	3,110.64	4,147.52	4,147.52	4,147.52	4,147.52	4,147.52
GROSS PROFIT:	12,894.36	12,894.36	17,192.48	17,192.48	17,192.48	17,192.48	17,192.48
OPERSTING EXPENSES:							
AUTOMIBILE	504.15	504.15	672.20	672.20	672.20	672.20	672.20
COLLECTIONS	168.06	168.06	224.08	224.08	224.08	224.08	224.08
DIRECT FUNERAL EXPENSES	336.12	336.12	448.16	448.16	448.16	448.16	448.16
FACILITIES & EQUIPMENT	840.27	840.27	1,120.36	1,120.36	1,120.36	1,120.36	1,120.36
GENERAL EXPENSES	840.27	840.27	1,120.36	1,120.36	1,120.36	1,120.36	1,120.36
PERSONAL EXPENSES	4,201.32	4,201.32	5,601.76	5,601.76	5,601.76	5,601.76	5,601.76
PROMOTION	11,320.75	11,320.75	15,094.34	15,094.34	15,094.34	15,094.34	15,094.34
TAXES	672.21	672.21	896.28	896.28	896.28	896.28	896.28
LAND LEASE	0.00	0.00	0.00	0.00	0.00	0.00	0.00
BUILDING LEASE	14,475.00	14,475.00	14,475.00	14,475.00	14,475.00	14,475.00	14,475.00
	33,358.15	33,358.15	39,652.54	39,652.54	39,652.54	39,652.54	39,652.54
NET INCOME, before taxes	(20,463.79)	(20,463.79)	(22,460.06)	(22,460.06)	(22,460.06)	(22,460.06)	(22,460.06)
ADD:depreciation expense	2,294.40	2,294.40	3,059.20	3,059.20	3,059.20	3,059.20	3,059.20
NET CASH FLOW	(18,169.39)	(18,169.39)	(19,400.86)	(19,400.86)	(19,400.86)	(19,400.86)	(19,400.86)

Appendix D — continued

	Month #1	Month #2	Month #3	Month #4	Month #5	Month #6	Month #7
MARKET SHARE INTERMENTS	29	29	29	30	30	350	
# OF FUNERAL SERVICES	5	5	5	6	6	53	
% OF MARKET SHARE	17.2%	17.2%	17.2%	20.0%	20.0%	15.1%	
CASKET & SERVICES	4,500.00	4,500.00	4,500.00	4,500.00	4,500.00		
REVENUE: FUNERAL CHARGES	11,250.00	11,250.00	11,250.00	13,500.00	13,500.00	119,250.00	42.2%
CASKET	11,250.00	11,250.00	11,250.00	13,500.00	13,500.00	119,250.00	42.2%
VAULTS	3,500.00	3,500.00	3,500.00	4,200.00	4,200.00	37,100.00	13.1%
CLOTHING, CARDS, ETC.	675.00	675.00	675.00	810.00	810.00	7,155.00	2.5%
	26,675.00	26,675.00	26,675.00	32,010.00	32,010.00	282,755.00	100.0%
COSTS PER SERVICE: CASKET COSTS	3,543.75	3,543.75	3,543.75	4,252.50	4,252.50	37,563.75	13.28%
VAULT COSTS	1,401.75	1,401.75	1,401.75	1,682.10	1,682.10	14,858.55	5.25%
MISC. COSTS	238.90	238.90	238.90	286.68	286.68	2,532.34	0.90%
	5,184.40	5,184.40	5,184.40	6,221.28	6,221.28	54,954.64	19.44%
GROSS PROFIT:	21,490.60	21,490.60	21,490.60	26,825.60	25,788.72	227,800.36	80.56%
OPERSTING EXPENSES: AUTOMIBILE	840.25	840.25	840.25	1,008.30	1,008.30	8,906.65	3.15%
COLLECTIONS	280.10	280.10	280.10	336.12	336.12	2,969.06	1.05%
DIRECT FUNERAL EXPENSES	560.20	560.20	560.20	672.24	672.24	5,938.12	2.10%
FACILITIES & EQUIPMENT	1,400.45	1,400.45	1,400.45	1,680.54	1,680.54	14,844.77	5.25%
GENERAL EXPENSES	1,400.45	1,400.45	1,400.45	1,680.54	1,680.54	14,844.77	5.25%
PERSONAL EXPENSES	7,002.20	7,002.20	7,002.20	8,402.64	8,402.64	74,223.32	26.25%
PROMOTION	18,867.92	18,867.92	18,867.92	22,641.51	22,641.51	200,000.00	70.73%
TAXES	1,120.35	1,120.35	1,120.35	1,344.42	1,344.42	11,875.71	4.20%
LAND LEASE	0.00	0.00	0.00	0.00	0.00	0.00	0.00%
BUILDING LEASE	14,475.00	14,475.00	14,475.00	14,475.00	14,475.00	173,700.00	61.43%
	45,946.92	45,946.92	45,946.92	52,241.31	52,241.31	507,302.40	179.41%
NET INCOME, before taxes	(24,456.32)	(24,456.32)	(24,456.32)	(25,415.71)	(26,452.59)	(279,502.04)	-98.85%
ADD:depreciation expense	3,824.00	3,824.00	3,824.00	4,588.80	4,588.80	40,534.40	14.34%
NET CASH FLOW	(20,632.32)	(20,632.32)	(20,632.32)	(20,826.91)	(21,863.79)	(238,967.64)	-84.51%

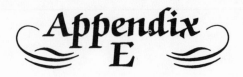

Appendix E

CEO Control Sheet

This is a hand posted sheet for and by Top Managers

This monthly report or something like it, using categories that make sense in your operation, should be hand posted by the CEO The computer has removed top management from close involvement with the people and numbers they work with, department to department. Hand posting and personal gathering of the figures is designed to keep selected operational numbers in the mind of the manager.

1. Number of Interments: _____
2. Number of Entombments: _____
3. Number of Cremations: _____
4. Number of Funerals _____
5. Pre-Need Volume:
    Cemetery _____
    Funerals _____
6. Trust/Insurance Balances:
    Funeral _____
    Care Fund _____
    Merchandise _____
7. Pre-need cash down-payments:
    Cemetery _____
    Funeral _____
8. At-Need Sales:
    Cemetery _____
    Funeral _____
9. Gross Receipts:
    Cemetery _____
    Funeral Home _____
    Flower Shop _____
10. Total Disbursements:
    Cemetery _____
    Funeral Home _____
    Flower Shop _____

11. Functional profit: _____

12. Memorial installations, number:
    Single _____
    Companion _____
    Monuments _____

13. Number of memorials to be
    installed: _____

14. Repurchases:
    Ground _____
    Mausoleum/Garden Crypt _____
    Other _____

15. Disinterments: _____

16. Sections personally walked: _____

17. Inventory:
    Caskets _____
    Vaults _____
    Granite bases _____

18. Number of department
    heads meetings: _____

19. Number of supervisor meetings: _____

20. Number of quality circle meetings: _____

21. Bank Balances:
    Bank C _____
    Bank F _____

22. Personnel-Ground: F_____ P_____
    Funeral Home _____
    Sales, P/N/C/ _____
    Flower Shop _____
    General and administration _____

23. Number of full time – total: _____

24. Number of part time – total: _____

Appendix F

Salespeople and Sales Management

Interview Check List

Ratings: Scale is 1-5, with 5 being best rating. All listings are considered attributes.

This unempirical rating scale helps classify important issues. Fill this out after the interview...not during.

Top Score Possible – 50   Cut off – 25

Verbal Facility _____

Word Choice _____

Thick Skinned _____

Stubborn _____

Appearance _____

Resilient _____

Open Personality _____

Friendly _____

Listener _____

Inter-Personal Skills _____

Appendix G

Price Protection Modular Payment Plan

Amount	12 Months	24 Months	36 Months	48 Months	60 Months
A.P.R.	14.010	14.237	14.120	13.930	13.723
$1,000	$ 89.79	$ 48.12	$ 34.23	$ 27.29	
$1,250	$ 112.22	$ 60.14	$ 42.78	$ 34.10	$ 28.89
$1,500	$ 134.68	$ 72.18	$ 51.35	$ 40.93	$ 34.68
$1,750	$ 157.11	$ 84.20	$ 59.90	$ 47.74	$ 40.45
$2,000	$ 179.58	$ 96.24	$ 68.47	$ 54.58	$ 46.24
$2,250	$ 202.01	$ 108.27	$ 77.02	$ 61.39	$ 52.01
$2,500	$ 224.47	$ 120.31	$ 85.58	$ 68.22	$ 57.81
$2,750	$ 246.90	$ 132.33	$ 94.13	$ 75.03	$ 63.58
$3,000	$ 269.37	$ 144.37	$ 102.70	$ 81.87	$ 69.37
$3,250	$ 291.80	$ 156.39	$ 111.25	$ 88.68	$ 75.14
$3,500	$ 314.26	$ 168.43	$ 119.82	$ 95.52	$ 80.93
$3,750	$ 336.69	$ 180.45	$ 128.37	$ 102.33	$ 86.70
$4,000	$ 359.16	$ 192.49	$ 136.94	$ 109.16	$ 92.49
$4,250	$ 381.59	$ 204.51	$ 145.49	$ 115.97	$ 98.26
$4,500	$ 404.06	$ 216.56	$ 154.06	$ 122.81	$ 104.06
$4,750	$ 426.49	$ 228.58	$ 162.61	$ 129.62	$ 109.83
$5,000	$ 448.95	$ 240.62	$ 171.17	$ 136.45	$ 115.62

Downpayments should be in amounts of $250.00. Example: $250, $500, $750, $1,000, etc. And if that isn't possible, use your regular payment book that you've used in the past. Please note the purpose of this program is to protect the prices on products and services they have not purchased yet. For example: 2 spaces are $1,000. By purchasing the 2 spaces, they have protected the price on the rest of the package. In this case, it would be price protection on a marker for $1,000, 2 opening and closings for $750. Price protection means the retail price cannot go up over 5% per year.

Approval:_____

CEO.

GLOSSARY

Assistant to: (Or, in many cases, the executive secretary.) A person publicly unassailable outside the private office of the boss, this person is frequently nepotic (see nepotism).

At-Need: This term is used when there has been a death, and property or other merchandise is needed now.

Barracuda: A term for the person in the firm who eats people and ideas that threaten or come from the wrong person, even when the idea is superior. Insatiable appetite.

Basket: An arrangement of flowers either in metal, plastic or wicker baskets.

Bier: A platform that the casket is placed on for display during visitation and funeral services.

Board of Directors: Also known as trustees as well as other terms too numerous to mention. When they appear, they are treated as EXALTED. Exception: when the employee is a member of the board. Function is to try, with a pile of papers issued at the time of the meeting, to act as though they know what is going on and how to vote in any way not indicated by the presenter, usually the general manager, who has done his homework (self preservation). Occasionally gets hold of a thread the GM did not anticipate and takes a great deal of time and glee in riding that horse, only to back off after he has shown his teeth. Never one to rock the boat in a final way. *Exception:* where the above is not true and where the Board is on the ball and kept up to date by the GM.

Budgets: Financial planning vehicles. What will happen, based on what has happened. Adjusted by changes in the firm's accent and direction. Otherwise, a non-existent one of the above.

Burial Vault: A concrete, metal or fiber glass container into which a casket is placed for burial. The purpose is to protect the casket from the weight of the earth.

Casket Pall: A cloth that drapes the casket during visitation or the funeral. The pall is used by some religious faiths, or can be an American flag. Also, it could be a floral arrangement placed on the casket during visitation and the funeral. It is also called a casket spray or casket cover.

CEO The person who oversees all divisions except one. This is always true. If there are four divisions, he/she will be up on three and the other runs itself. Since the CEO is good at what he/she does, the division he/she ignores is easy to see (smell, etc.).

Certified Copy of Death Certificate: A copy of a death certificate that is certified to be a true copy of the original. A certified copy is identified by the seal of the Health Department and signature of an employee of the Health Department.

Columbarium: An area in a mausoleum or other structure containing recesses (Niches) used to contain and sometimes display urns of cremated remains.

Companion/Companion Couch: Crypts side by side for companion burial. Caskets will be place lengthwise (feet first) in a companion and sideways for companion couch.

Concrete Box: A concrete container for the casket that is designed to protect the casket from weight of the earth, but offers no protection against the entrance of moisture.

Consultant: The temporarily unemployed. He/she was either fired or elected too soon to go it on his own. Exception: very few, but there are consultants that are very professional and who do not have an outside source of income. Usually marry well the second time if not the first.

COO: In charge of day-to-day operations. Cannot afford to ignore any division. Generally is the organization's *glue*.

Cremation: The reduction of human remains to bone fragments by intense heat.

Cremation Tray: A soft wood or corrugated receptacle used in lieu of a casket to cover and contain the remains until the time of cremation.

Crematory: Chamber in which human remains are cremated. Also, referred to as *retort*.

Crypt: This is the concrete space for casket placement.

Death Certificate: A legal document listing statistical information about a deceased person and stipulating the cause of death as certified by a physician. It is the funeral home's responsibility to file this document with the local Department of Health.

Deed/Certificate of Ownership: This a certificate issued to all new property owners after the contract has been paid in full. This certificate gives the owner *right of interment only*. The property is not owned outright. The certificate is issued on lots and mausoleum showing the exact location of the property. The certificate does not include the purchase of merchandise or services.

Delegate: The ability to. One who does this has confidence. One who does not, has much to do. This is the breeding grounds for procrastinators.

Delegation of Authority: Letting others perform tasks that should not occupy the top manager. In small firms, this is entirely academic. In larger firms, this is usually under done, if not over done. This is very hard to do correctly.

Department Heads: Non-existent in smaller (one man gang) firms. Otherwise, these are the operating bosses of the separate divisions.

Desks: For salespeople, a place to look busy, and hone the art of prospect card solitaire. For the secretary, a place to leave for a break. For the boss, a barrier that protects and, when large enough, intimidates. For the grounds superintendent, a surface to not clean or have seen. For him it must be covered, totally.

Direct Cremation: Cremation without viewing the remains or having any memorial service.

Double Depth Burial: This term refers to two persons interred in one space.

Emblems: These are small bronze plaques placed on markers, monuments or crypt fronts. Examples: club or lodge emblems, or religious emblems such as a cross or open Bible.

Entombment: This is the act of burying the deceased in a crypt.

Errors: Incorrect moves performed by subordinates. Attention is called to these. All shall know.

Executive Committee: The dumping ground for any issue that needs attention but is perplexing management. Use is, "Our executive committee is discussing this at the present time and will handle the matter." Actually, otherwise, a potentially very useful group.

File: A place for memos; also see wastebaskets.

Funeral Trust: An agreement with the purchaser to supply a complete funeral service, including casket, for a price set by current day standards. The money collected from this agreement is held in a trust until the death of the individual and at the time is withdrawn from the trust to pay for the funeral service. Any interest which has been added to the account helps to off-set the additional cost to the funeral home at the time of the service.

Garden Mausoleum: This is the same as a mausoleum with the only difference being that the crypts are outside.

Gravesite Service: Funeral service that is held at the grave site rather than in the funeral home or church.

Inscription: This is the name and date of birth and death of the deceased, placed on the front of the crypt, marker or monument.

Interment or Opening & Closing: This is the act of burying a person in the ground. We charge a fee for this service, separate from the burial space.

Lawn Crypts: This term is applied to spaces designed in which the casket is placed at the time of interment. Usually double depth. These are below ground, pre-installed concrete containers for the interment of human remains.

Mausoleum: This is an above ground structure and the burial is made inside the building.

Memorial Service: A service conducted in memory of the deceased, most often following cremation, with or without the remains being present.

Nepotic: A coined expression, meaning "family member."

Nepotism: The act of being nepotic. To employ the kin in the business. Non- relatives tend to not rise above the family members. Another form is to employ a married couple, not in the family of owners. This is thought to be a bad form of nepotism, while the family variety is accepted. Where the total number of employees equals the total number of family members, we have no problem, only a concept to discuss.

Niche: The space which holds cremated remains. This can be glass front niches or wood front niches, marble or granite. Glass front niches contain urns which are engraved; wood front niches will have inscriptions on the front, similar to the crypt fronts.

Origination Fee: This is a charge to all new property owners for the recording, processing and deeding of property. This is also charged funeral families for administrative functions.

Paranoia: Fear. "Wonder what he meant by that?" is an example. Price changers, direction changers. The paranoid person may well be pure in operations and wonder what he did or said that has been misinterpreted.

Placement Time: The time set as the starting point of a funeral home visitation.

Pre-Need: This term is used when property and other cemetery or funeral home merchandise has been purchased before a death.

Preparation Room: The rooms in the funeral home used for embalming and preparing the remains for visitation and funeral.

Presentation: The term used by the Sales Department to provide the family with facts about the advantages of purchasing.

Pro forma: Frequently thought of as a dart board. In actual fact, they are so easy to do, they are usually done correctly. But like computers, garbage in, garbage out. One of the major reasons consultants lose their clients (*see consultants*).

Public relations: Call your office and see how yours is handled. Ask a fairly off the wall question, such as, "How much does the funeral cost?" I hate to tell you what you will find out, but there will usually be a meeting, and soon (see assistant).

Quality circles: Identification for groups of employees helping to identify and solve problems.

Receptacle Any of the casket containers defined above.

Redden: A verb, "to make red."

Secrets: Incorrect moves performed by the boss. It's between him and his MAKER. The exception is at the boss's home. There he makes errors (*see errors*).

Sections/Blocks/Lots/Spaces: These are terms used to identify the grave locations of burials and property owned.

Stateroom: Rooms in the funeral home used specifically for visitation.

Supervisors: Work at the direction of the department heads. Line people, get the job done.

Tandem: Crypts placed end to end. The first burial is placed in the back and the second entombment directly in front.

T.P.A: Total Pre-Arrangement. This is where our families purchase everything necessary for complete cemetery arrangements in advance of death. Usually includes the lot, marker, interment charges and vault. This would include a mausoleum package with crypts, entombment and inscription.

Transfer: A form which must be completed and notarized to transfer property from one person to another. These forms are needed even to transfer from husband to wife or mother to daughter. An affidavit is often required.

Urn: A receptacle for holding remains which can be made of various materials: bronze, copper, wood, marble or cardboard

<u>Vault:</u> This refers to the outer receptacle in which the casket is placed at the time of interment.

<u>Visitation:</u> The time before a funeral service set aside for relatives and friends of the deceased to visit and usually view the remains. This is usually held the evening prior to the day of the funeral. Also referred to as (1) wake, (2) viewing and (3) lying in state.

<u>Wastebasket</u>: File for many unneeded items, including, but not limited to, memos.

Bibliography

Modern Cemetery Management
By G. J. Klupar
Catholic Cemeteries of the Archdiocese of Chicago
1962

NFDA Resource Manual
Howard C. Raether, J.D. Executive Editor
1984

Peopleography

Blame and fame to the friends who have played a part in my education and successes in the cemetery and funeral endeavors. Some used one method, some another. All taught me. Some didn't know it. Some aren't listed, they were too subtle.

Larry Anspach	One who shares.
Herchel Auerbach	Organization.
Dave Boyd	Buy, build and sell.
Jack Brammer	Judgement.
Harold Brown	Personal selling.
Ron Brooks.	Versatility.
Duane Broyles	Patience.
John Campbell	One-track selling.
Robert Carlson	Organization.
David Carmony	Conviction.
Frank Carney	A good attorney.
John Crerar	Staying aware.
J.D. Crouch	He's in the process of teaching.
B. David Daly	Overall excellence.
E.C. Daves	Appearances.
Vic Deacy	Company loyalty.
Bill Downey	Public relations concepts.
Danny Eaton	Desire and enthusiasm.
Jim Edwards	Grounds operations.
Pete Ernst	Value of a partner.
Cheryl Etheridge	Drive and convictions.
Jack Frost	How to juggle.
Tommy Gardner	Sales management and attitude.
Dan Garrison	Integrity and organization.
Loren Glock	Create.
Zolman Goldsmith	Yet another good attorney.
Dennis Hamilton	A profit-driven director.
Frank Hawkins	Personal selling.
Bill Henning	Decency.
Phil Herr	Funeral Director turned cemeterian.

Bob Herr	Caution.
Ed Hewlett	Funeral Director builds a cemetery.
J.D. Ingram	Quality.
Tim Iott	A CPA with a sense of humor.
Andy Jackson	A Funeral Director takes to sales.
Jay Joliat	Tops in investments.
Frank Karnes	Solid operations.
Julian Lackey	Determination.
Harvey Lapin	A dedicated attorney.
Shale Lapping	Versatility.
Lane Latimer	Friendship and finances.
Brad Leggett	Desire to achieve.
Harry Leggett Jr.	Family values.
Arch and Larry Long	Friendship's value
Jim Love	Ego strength.
Jex Luce	Operational tradition.
Robin Luce	Detail is important after all.
Reed Mabe	Personal selling.
Eric Mamorek	Excellence.
Doug Manuel	Liaison and administration.
Gail Manuel	Aggressive marketer.
Brian Marlow	Persistency.
Norman Marlowe	Stability personified.
Sam McClesky	Dependable-excellence.
Fred Meyer Jr.	Build.
Steve Morgan	Tough mindedness.
Jody Morris	Diplomacy.
M.N. Murray	Aggressiveness.
Asher Neel	Great trainer.
Robert Neel	Ideas and optimism.
Keith Norwalk	Aggressiveness in a new field.
Mark Nuckolls	Aggressive.
Ted Nuckolls	The Gold Cross high rise.
Bill Pailey	Creativity.
Dick Pennington	Direction of purpose.
Ed Phillips	Cultivation of relationships.

Dan Reed	An idea factory.
Darrell Roberts	Innovation.
Wayne Sanford	Public relations-historian.
Dick Schewe	True service.
David Scruggs	What a good attorney is.
Katherine Smythe	Provided my greatest challenge
Eric Spencer	Handling self with people.
Gene Stallings	What a good CPA looks like.
Frank Stewart	Building an organization.
Jim Stewart	Grounds operations.
Buzzie Stoecklein	A shaker and a mover.
George Stoecklein	First in the veterans marketing.
Gene Strong	Superb Architect.
Brewer "Buck" Thompson	Never quit learning.
Lon Thurmer	A gentleman Funeral Director.
H.E. Toson	My boss/mentor for the first six years in this work. He taught me to think and work all at the same time, without moving my lips.
H.N. Toson	I entered into the cemetery field because of him. Great friend.
Paul Vanderkolk	Best in sales management.
David Warmby	Thinking big.
Mary Wilder	Concentration.
Doc Williams	Boldness.
George Young	Great leader and innovator.

To steal from one is plagiarism; from many is research.

Index